Navigating the Labyrinth of the Non-Mainstream Child

By

Susan Hendrie-Marais

ISBN-13: 978-0692591581

Cover: Roman Mosaic Labyrinth,
c.200-250 CE
Conimbriga, Portugal

Photo by Jeff Saward
Labyrinthos Photo Library

DEDICATION

For my mother, whose boundless optimism, energy, and resourcefulness have kept me moving forward, always.

For my son, who never ceases to challenge and impress me.

Table of Contents

Table of Contents

List of Tables

List of Tables

AUTHOR'S NOTE

In my thinking and doing I had the benefit of significant, essentially unlimited, resources to address the problems I describe in this book. I recognize that this will not be the case for most people, and as a result they may not be able to do the things I did in the way that I did them, or possibly at all. Notwithstanding this, I believe this book can still be valuable as one person's attempt at "best practices" for how to think about and manage the problems that special needs children and their families face. It is the book I wish I had read before I embarked on this journey. Where possible I have added strategies, potential funding sources, and options for navigating this labyrinth in a more affordable manner.

Susan Hendrie-Marais
May 22, 2016
Mill Valley, California

I. FIRST YOU PANIC, BUT YOU DON'T HAVE TO

If your experience is like mine, one day, in your otherwise uneventful life, you will have received the shocking news that your child's development is not meeting the milestones that some authority somewhere has decided were a prerequisite for normal, healthy growth.

You probably will have wondered already about the sometimes odd behaviors of your child. Maybe the lack of eye contact or the repeated, perseverative, phrases and gestures. Maybe the intense fixation on certain inanimate objects. You may have attributed these oddities to genes from the brilliant but eccentric man you married or other various unique family circumstances. In fact, you have now been told that there is "something wrong," that the gestures and behaviors you once found oddly charming are evidence of some kind of developmental problem, a delay, disorder, or God knows what.

What now?

After taking a really deep breath and some time to compose myself, what I did was to try to figure out what this was, what it meant, and what I could and should be doing about it. This book is a chronicle of that journey; the knowledge I gained, the mistakes I made, and the advice I wish someone had given me. I am by no means an authority in any of the areas relevant to these problems. I have two science degrees and an MBA, none of these even close to the knowledge of the medical and mental health professionals we came to know so well. I have not worked in health care or in any of the mental health fields. I was then, and am now, a really devoted, tenacious, and neurotic mom trying to figure out how to help my wonderful but sometimes troubled child. The good news is you don't have to panic, but you do have to think hard and work even harder from here on in.

II. WHAT TO DO FIRST: FRAMING YOUR THINKING

One of the most powerful things I learned in my many years of graduate school was that to solve a problem you first have to define what that problem is and what it is not, in other words, where it starts and where it ends. This is called setting the initial boundary conditions and is one of the most important things you will need to think about in the murky world into which you have been thrown. It will come up in the following way. Let's say you've been told that your child has a visual processing disorder, which means that their brain has difficulty interpreting what it sees. It is important to know if this is also a problem with vision, and/or a functional problem in the brain, such as an inability to integrate visual information. Each of these will have its own associated consequences and effects, which you will also want to understand. In our case, our pediatrician was concerned that my son was not speaking by his third birthday. Most boys are speaking by age three and girls typically even earlier. My son clearly understood language, which meant that his receptive language was fine, but not speaking meant that there might be something wrong with his expressive language. I say might because there are exceptions, and sometimes a child's development is delayed without an associated problem. We were encouraged to see an audiologist for hearing tests and then, when no hearing problem was found, to see speech therapists. The speech therapists worked with my son for several months before they decided that they were worried about the nature of his social interactions. He had his own single-minded agenda, did not really care what the adults around him thought, did not seek approval, and was intensely focused on the aspects of the world that he found interesting, with little concern for much else. Such focused single mindedness violated the accepted norms for social behavior in toddlers. The speech therapists recommended we see a behavioral pediatrician and from there my story starts.

Figuring out what and where your child's problems are is crucial. To make matters even more difficult, the problems are dynamic, they will change over time, either getting better or worse relative to where they were at the start or where they should be. You might, for example, find that your child has an auditory processing weakness, or their speech is delayed, as we found. If there is an auditory processing weakness, this means that auditory information, or what is heard, is not fully received and/or processed by the brain. This can result in sounds not being completely understood. Without accurate hearing, the mimicry that is essential to language learning may not happen in the way it is supposed to, or may not happen at all. Over time, an auditory processing weakness could evolve into a speech disorder or delay and the speech delay then could have a cascade of effects such as difficulty with social interactions at school. One child we knew was always falling off playground equipment and bumping into other children at school. He often mistakenly punched other children, not having a good sense of the length of his arm and where his fists were in the space around him. What started as clumsiness was first treated as a problem with his vision. He was given glasses and told to do special eye exercises to improve his sight. He then seemed to have difficulty in school distinguishing shapes and letters. This resulted in difficulty learning to read and write and he was then diagnosed as dyslexic. [1] Finally, a visual processing disorder was detected, or maybe was always there. [2] The boy could not orient himself in space and did not have a good sense of objects and their physical relationship to each other. Over time he had difficulty with more advanced math and was diagnosed with a

---

1. Dyslexia is a learning disability in which processing and understanding words and/or numbers is difficult, resulting in problems reading. It may also include problems with spelling, writing, and pronouncing words.

2. A visual processing disorder results in difficulty understanding visual information, copying figures, reading information at a distance, and navigating oneself through space.

nonverbal learning disorder. [3]

A good place to start thinking about the boundaries of your child's problem is with a developmental behavioral pediatrician. In my experience, most pediatricians have a limited knowledge of developmental issues. They will understand the developmental guidelines and milestones, which means what should be happening at what age, based on the medical community's experience (see Appendix A). Pediatricians generally do not, however, know much about what to do if your child does not meet one or more of these milestones. For example, they will know that at age two months your baby should be smiling, beginning to follow objects with their eyes and recognizing people, or at age three that they should be taking turns and showing concern for friends. A good pediatrician should notice if your child is not meeting a developmental milestone, which often will be the first sign of a developmental issue. In our case, our pediatrician noticed that my son was not speaking by age three.

Developmental behavioral pediatricians are pediatricians who have had training in the subspecialty of developmental-behavioral pediatrics. They will have an in-depth understanding of developmental issues and will be able to direct you to the appropriate specialists for additional testing, which will then begin to quantify what is happening. A behavioral pediatrician might see a child who is socially awkward and has difficulty reading social cues, or a child with a hyper-acute sensory system that makes him always on edge and anxious. Depending on the nature of your child's issues, there are a variety of tests that can give you more detailed understanding of what is problematic. These tests measure your child's performance against some norm or average level of function for children of roughly the same age (see Appendix B). There are four general

---

3. With a nonverbal learning disorder (NLD) a child's verbal skills are significantly stronger than their fine motor and visual-spatial skills. Children with NLD typically have difficulty with math and hand writing. They are often extremely bright and also struggle with social skills and paying attention. NLD is also called a nonverbal learning disability.

areas in which developmental skills are tested:

- Cognitive Function, such as problem solving and learning
- Fine and Gross Motor Skills
- Language and Communication Skills
- Personal and Social Skills

The choice of test is based on the problems being screened for, your child's culture, and the cost, time, and difficulty of administering the test ("Identifying Infants and Young Children" 416).

Developmental testing, or screening, can be fantastically expensive, running into thousands of dollars. With Obamacare, some developmental tests are now covered as preventive care. These include autism screening for children 18 to 24 months, behavioral assessments for children to age 17, and depression screening in adolescents. Developmental testing can also be covered under Medicare, providing the correct diagnostic and procedure (CPT) [4] codes and the required paperwork are filed by your pediatrician or whoever is administering the tests. You should keep a record of the CPT and diagnostic codes used for your child; you will need them for future insurance questions.

A behavioral pediatrician, like other specialists and therapists, is expensive, particularly if your child needs ongoing care, which means ongoing appointments. Some providers will have sliding scales. This means that for children from families with lower incomes they will have a lower fee, with the fee increasing as family income becomes higher. It is worth asking whether a specialist works on a sliding scale, as they may not mention this when you first speak to them. Sometimes

---

4. See "What are CPT Codes."
http://patients.about.com/od/costsconsumerism/a/cptcodes.htm.
CPT codes are written on your invoices by your doctor or specialist. There will be a code for each procedure or service performed and a diagnostic code as well. All are important and may change over time.

specialists will be clear at the onset about how they charge for their services. For example, at my first meeting with one new psychiatrist, I was asked our family's income. I found this weird and uncomfortable, until I asked why this was relevant to our conversation about my son. The psychiatrist explained that he had a sliding scale, so families could afford to work with him regardless of their income.

There are resources. A number of private funding sources provide grants to families whose children have special needs. These are easy to find on the net by googling something like, "funding for special needs children." Your local Community Mental Health Center should also have specialists and testing services available, often at a much more affordable price. The center close to you can be found online using the Substance Abuse and Mental Health Services Administration (SAMHA) Behavioral Health Treatment Service Locator. Advocacy organizations such as The National Alliance on Mental Illness (NAMI) and Mental Health America (MHA) also help families find services. NAMI has vowed to "advocate at all levels to ensure (persons who need them) …receive the services they need…in a timely fashion" ("NAMI Mission"). If you have a university or college near to you that offers graduate programs in psychology, psychiatry, counseling, social work, or therapy, another possible option is to inquire whether there is a clinic associated with these programs. At such clinics, graduate students, with supervision, often provide services to the community at dramatically reduced prices or for free, as a final part of their training.

Your public school is a source of services and specialists once your child is in school. Federal law requires that all public schools provide "a free and appropriate education in the least restrictive environment possible" ("Services in Schools"), which includes testing for developmental issues. If testing indicates that your child is eligible for services, an Individual Education Plan (IEP) is then written by the school, with your participation and the participation of any specialists or advisors you want to bring to this conversation. The IEP details the therapists and services your child is entitled to under the law. Examples of services that might be included are speech therapy, occupational therapy, physical therapy, sessions with a psychologist, and/or a classroom aide. If you do not feel an IEP is appropriate or adequate for your child, you have the right to appeal, and there are resources and organizations available to help you. [5] If your public school is not able to provide the appropriate services and specialists, they are required by federal law to pay for an alternative school venue, which includes private schools that might better meet your child's needs. Public school services, however, unfortunately do not begin until your child enters public school. Ideally, you would like to uncover and begin working on any developmental weaknesses much earlier.

Obamacare has created another option. It requires insurers to provide mental health benefits equal in kind and amount to those provided for physical healthcare. It also requires that prior conditions no longer be excluded. Your child's specialists and therapists should thus be covered by your insurance, providing that you can show that a given service is "medically necessary." Medical necessity can be proven by a letter from your physician stating that the services in question are necessary, an explanation as to why, and a diagnostic code. If the insurance company declines to cover the expenses, you have the option of requesting a medical review to contest this decision. In my experience, if you are persistent, you generally can get the insurance company to pay for at least part and often a significant portion of the cost for these services.

Once you have gotten developmental test results it is important to remember that these results are not necessarily absolute. Even if your child's scores indicate that they are below the "normal" range, results can often be open to interpretation. We were told, for example, that based on testing my son would have difficulty reading and writing. This never happened. He was able to both read and write with no more difficulty than any other child his age. Eventually his handwriting was amongst the

---

5. Online resources offering information on how to manage IEP appeals and problems include the websites UnderstandingSpecialEd.com, specialed.about.com/od/iep/a/ Due-Process-How-Parents-Assert-Their-Rights.htm.

best in his class. After speaking to enough people and looking at enough test results, you will begin to get an idea of what's going on and what areas of your child's functioning are affected. The next step is to enlist the help of specialists in the areas of concern. For example, your child might need speech therapists, (also called speech pathologists), if there are problems with language, communication, pragmatic, or social skills, such as how to start a conversation with a peer or how to better articulate sounds. A physical therapist might be needed if your child has problems with movement and fine motor skills, such as jumping, writing, or drawing. If your child has difficulty with coordination and daily life tasks, such as dressing or tying shoes, an occupational therapist might be called. A psychologist, counselor, social worker, or psychiatrist might be needed for emotional and psychological issues. For example, depression, anxiety, or obsessive-compulsive behavior. It is essential to find good doctors and therapists to help you. These medical providers will be your window into what is and what is not functioning well in your child and how to intervene to support them as much as possible through the consequences.

Related to defining the boundaries of your child's issues is trying to understand the causes. Ideally, you would like to have any treatment you pursue address causes and not just symptoms. For example, if your child is anxious, it is important to understand if there is something in his environment causing the anxiety, such as a mean classmate, a harsh teacher, or difficulty doing his schoolwork. Alternatively, anxiety can be due to something internal and organic. For example, it could be a biochemical, neurological, and/or psychological problem, all intrinsic to your child by virtue of genetic inheritance or some other biological origin. A child born into a family of highly anxious and compulsive overachievers, for example, is likely to be anxious and compulsive. In such cases, the anxiety would be inherited and internal and then reinforced externally by interactions with anxious siblings and parents at home. If the underlying cause of a child's issues is internal, a change in the environment will usually not be enough to fundamentally change the condition. With our example, moving to another class or different school might help some, but if the child's anxiety is internal, these sorts of external changes will not be adequate to fundamentally improve the child's well-being. The underlying anxiety condition would likely persist.

Often a child's problem is due to a combination of internal and external causes. One child we knew completely shut down in school, sitting mute and unresponsive on the floor for most of the day. A therapist discovered that the boy's brother and his friends had been teasing him about a recent growth spurt that had made him tall and really thin. A set of external circumstances, the teasing, disturbed the boy enough to trigger an underlying and internal anxiety condition. Sometimes the causality is reversed. An internal, intrinsic condition can cause the external environment to become hostile. An anxious girl begins to wring her hands and pace around on the playground at school. Seeing this, other children think she is weird and begin to tease her. She is ostracized, which then increases her anxiety; she paces more, and a self-reinforcing cycle is created. Whether the cause is primarily intrinsic and internal or external is important to understand. Problems emanating from external causes can often be remedied by making changes in your child's environment. You can change a classroom or school to get your child away from bullying peers much more easily than you can affect anxiety stemming from an underlying biochemical or genetic issue. For the boy who shut down in school, once someone spoke to his brother and his friends, they stopped teasing him. As a result, his anxiety was reduced and he was able to function in a typical, healthy manner. His internal anxiety condition was mild enough to be quelled by an external change. He will probably always be vulnerable to having his anxiety triggered by stress and will have to be careful. In the case of the hand wringing girl, her anxiety was more profound and due to internal causes; it would not be eliminated or reduced much by a change in external conditions, such as a new school. Her condition will persist regardless of the environment, although some circumstances might be easier for her to manage than others. Intrinsic, internal causes usually result in a recommendation for some sort of medication. Sometimes, both external environmental changes and medication are the answer. Understanding the problem, if you can, is thus essential, as it will guide you to the most effective treatment. I would question any professional who does not seriously and thoughtfully pursue your child's symptoms backwards towards a theory as to what the cause might be and why. They often will not know the answer, and it is to their credit if they have the confidence to admit this, but they should have some hypothesis, hopefully based on careful thinking about your child's symptoms and what is known about your child's world. This is, however, not always the case. My son saw a pediatrician who headed a prestigious child development center and was reputed to be an excellent diagnostician. After what seemed like endless, expensive, and time-consuming sessions with her staff, and an initial session with her, she sent us a report that appeared to be little more than a standardized summary with my son's name at the top. There was no thinking about my son's individual circumstances, no attempt to understand what the causes were and why, just a pro forma, "here's what we found and here is generally what this means." Evaluations such as these are emotionally wrenching. To receive a report that read as if it could have applied to just about any child with developmental issues made me furious. I contacted the specialist, the head of her department, and the head of the hospital in which she worked and complained that her work was unacceptable. No one said a word. I never received a call to speak about what had happened, and also was never sent a bill. We then found a new pediatrician.

Often the cause of childhood developmental problems is not clear and what you will get is hypothesis and speculation. This is actually ok, as you can triage between or amongst several professionals who approach the problem from different perspectives towards a plausible cause that seems right to you and consistent with what you know. For example, both a cognitive behavioral psychologist and a psychodynamic psychiatrist might see a child with phobias. The cognitive behavioral psychologist might see the problem as resulting from an internal tendency to exaggerate danger that over time conditioned the child to imagine the worst possible outcome and to respond with fearful, phobic behaviors. The treatment might consist of substituting healthier behaviors for the conditioned the classroom when classmates entered after lunch, for example, the psychologist might help the child learn to breathe deeply and visualize something empowering, which would then enable them to stay in the room. Over time, the child would hopefully learn to generalize this healthier response to their entire world.

A psychodynamic psychiatrist would likely approach the problem of phobias as an unconscious, internal conflict. A repressed emotion resulting from this conflict might have created the phobias. The therapeutic focus would be to understand the conflicts and their early childhood origins. In this paradigm, for example, the child might have developed phobias as a result of repressed feelings of inadequacy that resulted from early childhood interactions with an excessively critical parent. The psychiatrist would try to take the child back to early memories of these interactions to help them understand how these interactions caused the phobic behaviors. Combining the perspectives of these two specialists, you could learn about both the origins of your child's phobic behaviors and the hierarchy of feelings and thoughts behind them. Hopefully then you could begin to define the scope and cause of the problem.

After many years in this world, I have come to understand that childhood development is not well understood when it veers off the mainstream and follows its own unique course. There are no benchmarks. This is especially true for issues having to do with cognitive function and mental health. Often the only thing a medical professional can do is to treat symptoms after guessing at a cause. As you speak to more professionals, you will begin to develop your own theories as to what is causing your child's issues and what interventions seem to be the most effective. You should trust your intuition. You are the only person who knows your child across the entire spectrum of their life. It is your job to coordinate and integrate what you see and hear over time into a coherent picture.

In summary, the initial foundations of your thinking should be the answers to the following questions:

1. What is the scope of my child's issues?
2. What areas of my child's development are affected?

3. What are the possible causes?
4. What can I do to help?

Everything you think and do should flow from the search to answer these questions. And these are the questions you should keep coming back to as your child moves forward.

III. WHAT TO DO NEXT

The next step is to find professionals who can help. You will need to understand what kinds of specialists and therapies your child needs and then choose people to work with in each area. You probably first heard about these issues from your pediatrician. They should be able to recommend a developmental behavioral pediatrician who can then do a more in-depth assessment of your child's development and recommend any needed follow up. A developmental behavioral pediatrician is not a requirement in this process but is helpful as an advisor across the entire spectrum of your child's development. They will understand who does what and which sorts of interventions are appropriate. A good developmental behavioral pediatrician should be helpful in giving you the beginning of an overall understanding of what is happening and how best to intervene to help. They should be knowledgeable about the therapies and interventions that could be relevant to your child's issues, specialists who can help, and the appropriate testing. Working with a developmental behavioral pediatrician turned my fuzzy ball of undefined concern and worry into a coherent plan for how to move forward. I came to understand that our problems were much more complicated than a speech delay and that they had odd, inexplicable spikes. There were complicated weaknesses in sensory regulation and visual-spatial perception, for example, but formidable language aptitude. The time I spent with this doctor felt much like creating a giant grid on which potential diagnostic categories were posted temporarily, analyzed, and subsequently either discarded as non-issues or pursed as areas of concern.

It is totally valid to proceed without the help of a developmental behavioral pediatrician, and this is obviously much less expensive. If you do this, you are then embarking on a bottom-up instead of a top-down approach. You can start with one specialist, such as a speech or physical therapist, see how things go, and then gradually add additional specialists and/or interventions as needed. Parents who first learn of their child's developmental issues when their child enters school often end up working this way. A teacher will notice something, send a child to the resource center for testing and evaluation, and the child might then begin working with a school specialist. Or, your pediatrician might notice something and send you to a therapist to have your child tested. You will get a more limited perspective from a specialist then you would from a generalist, such as a developmental behavioral pediatrician, but an experienced specialist can be remarkably wise about what a child needs and where a child's weaknesses lie. With a bottom-up approach, you will come to your integrated perspective later rather then sooner. Instead of starting out with every resource that might be needed, you will gradually work your way towards this point on an as-needed basis. Which approach you choose is a matter of personal preference. Both will get you to the same goal, which is to have a good group of specialists working with you and your child.

Once you understand which specialists you need and hopefully have been given names to pursue, you will then have to decide with whom you want to work. Physician and therapist bios can usually be found online. If they are on staff at a hospital it is especially easy, as the hospital website will have a section on its staff and their credentials. I always checked where any specialist I was considering went to undergraduate and medical or graduate school and where they did their subsequent training such as internships, residencies, and fellowships. My reasoning was that one has to do well in college to get into a respectable medical or graduate school, and similarly one has to do well in medical or graduate school to get into a good internship, residency, or fellowship program. All else being equal, and sometimes it isn't, I would rather work with someone who has done well in school and after. As with everything there are exceptions, and you will come across excellent professionals whose training is not impressive, but as doctors and therapists they are wonderful and you will not be able to do without them.

If you still need additional recommendations, calling

doctors you trust to ask for referrals is often helpful. Word of mouth can be helpful as well, particularly if someone you trust has actually seen the specialist in question and likes them. Googling something like, "best (whatever the specialist you need) in (the closest large city to you)" can also work, although you will then have to figure out which of the many lists that come up is worth pursuing. I always felt most comfortable using lists from organizations I had some familiarity with, such as U.S. News and World Report, Healthgrades, The New York Times, et cetera.

You can also go to the website of hospitals near you. Hospitals will have a roster of therapists and physicians who work there, or are affiliated, by specialty. You can read through the staff bios until you find someone whose research and/or specialty is relevant to your child's issues and then can look further to see where they went to medical or graduate school and where they did their residency or post graduate work and subsequent fellowships. If you need to determine where the good programs are for a given specialty, in psychiatry, for example, this can easily be done by googling something like, "best (or top) psychiatry programs." There will be multiple lists, and again, I always tried to use a source I liked or at least have heard of. You can do the same for graduate or medical schools and undergraduate colleges. Similarly, this works for foreign trained doctors, although the source lists may be from places you have never heard of before now. If you persevere, certain schools and programs will come up repeatedly and it is reasonable to assume that this means something.

The Internet can give you an idea of the specialist/professional landscape near you and can also tell you what is known about and has been done in your child's areas of concern. Interesting hospital or clinic programs, research at universities, hospitals and laboratories, who is doing what and where they are doing it should all be there. You can also get an idea as to where people you are considering fit in the web of providers available around you. Some names will come up repeatedly and are sometimes worth pursuing further. Other names will be on lists with less than favorable reviews. Your goal here is to try to get an idea of who and what is out there and who and what to stay away from.

Finally, I liked to check Yelp, Vitals, or other general review sites, to see what people said about specialists I was considering. Parents' networks can also be a good source of information and you don't have to limit yourself to networks in your area, as they are often online. The Berkeley Parents Network is a wealth of information, as I am sure others are as well. Who you work with is ultimately a subjective decision. You cannot always know whom you are getting beforehand, but you can at least know the information that is publicly available about them.

IV. WHAT NOT TO DO

Try to pick good people to work with and stay with them. Try not to change providers once your child has started with one person, unless something seems really wrong or your child's needs and/or issues change. Sometimes seeing additional therapists is useful temporarily to clarify some aspect of or question about your child's issues. For example, my son's third grade teacher noticed that he seemed to have difficulty focusing on pages of densely written information. Our pediatrician recommended that we see an eye specialist, who examined my son and concluded that the muscles in his eyes were weak. This made focusing for long periods of time difficult and tiring. The specialist gave him exercises to do at home and after several weeks he was done.

You should try to narrow down the set of providers you plan to work with on an ongoing basis as soon as possible. All else being equal, having your therapists and doctors see your child regularly over an extended period of time gives them more information and better insight into what is happening. It also enables you, your child, and the provider to develop a working rapport and become comfortable with one another.

There is a phenomenon called "diagnosis shopping," in which a parent searches for specialists who will give their child either the diagnosis the parent feels is correct, or the diagnosis that is most benign. During the many hours I spent in the waiting room of my son's speech therapists, I would often hear moms telling stories of their hunt for the doctor who could really "get" their child and have the one crucial insight that would make everything understandable. They would often travel to three and four or more different specialists, hoping the next evaluation would uncover the one crucial detail that would change everything. The mother of one autistic child had business cards made up with all of her personal information, so that she didn't have to keep giving her details to receptionists as she went from doctor to doctor looking for new insights and diagnoses. On her cards, below her name, in the space in which people typically put their profession, she had printed "truck driver," which I never completely understood but assume was a reference to always being on the road with her child.

Based on everything I have said to this point, shopping for a diagnosis may sound reasonable, but it isn't. At this point, you should be developing a point of view, testing that perspective, and pushing it forward. The fallacy in looking for specialists to confirm a diagnosis or theory that you believe is right is that it is limiting; you are starting at what should be the endpoint. You will have given yourself a premature conclusion before you have even begun to gather the information you need to get to a good conclusion. You are not looking for conclusions at this point. You are looking for the most effective means to move your understanding forward. This means enlisting the most capable and knowledgeable people you can find. The questions you are trying to answer should be both open-ended and changing and likely will not yet have answers. There are exceptions of course, but most developmental problems are complicated and have little clarity at the onset. You are looking for good providers to help you think about how to move forward effectively and how to understand what is happening. If they have a different point of view, that may be a good thing and it is at least worth pursuing why. There are likely things you have not considered or don't know that inform the specialist's perspective. As long as you can come to a common understanding, which may mean you still don't agree on the preliminary diagnosis, but you do agree on how to proceed, it is worth going ahead if you feel the person is good. My son had one psychiatrist with whom I sparred all the time about potential explanations and corollaries for what we were seeing. We almost never agreed, but I trusted him completely and always felt that I had gained a better understanding of what was going on after we finished a conversation. In the end, despite much arguing, we were always able to agree on an approach.

The providers you choose to work with should be the best people you can find who you feel you can work with productively. You should expect to question and debate what they say and they should be comfortable with your doing so. You are looking to create an ongoing conversation about your child.

Once you have decided on a set of professionals, you need to develop a working relationship. If your child's specialists are to be effective they will need space in which to work and you will ultimately have to trust them. Don't stay with, or ideally don't start with, any specialist whom you feel you cannot eventually grow to trust. This being said, it is reasonable to expect regular reports on what is happening and on how your child is doing relative to where they were when they started and relative to where you hope they can be. You will have to strike a balance between being well informed and reassured and being overly intrusive and demanding. This is sometimes hard at the onset but is critically important. Once the relationship is underway, if you need additional reassurance beyond regular progress updates, then either you have chosen the wrong specialist, or you may need to look beyond your child's doctor or therapist to a friend or therapist of your own.

Don't be intimidated. You are after all a paying client and no matter how prominent the doctor or therapist you are seeing, your relationship should be collaborative. Ask lots of questions. Each piece of advice and information you get should fit into your growing understanding of what is going on with your child. If someone says something that seems odd or inconsistent with what you have been hearing and thinking to date, question it. Doctors and therapists are human, they make mistakes, sometimes their emotions get in the way, and sometimes, fortunately rarely, they act in ways that are not helpful at all and can even be destructive. You need to be able to feel comfortable working with these people to get the best care for your child. If someone is not listening, or does not seem to be thinking clearly, or is unwilling to take the time to answer your questions thoughtfully and explain what they think is happening in a manner that you can understand, then you need another doctor or therapist, no matter how famous or renowned that person might be. We briefly saw a pediatric neurologist in San Francisco who insisted on examining my infant son on a cold cement floor in chilly January. Later that day she called me to say briskly that my son was epileptic and needed to be on anti-seizure medicine. She told me that I should not worry because, "these medications often enhance cognitive function," and then said she had to go to a meeting, leaving me holding the phone, in shock at the other end of the line. When I googled the medication she wanted to prescribe, I found that it had profound side effects, which for an infant would have been life changing. The combination of the phone call, medication recommendation, and exams on the cold floor made me realize that we needed another neurologist. Without looking very hard I was able to find a wonderful Senegalese neurologist across the bay at Oakland Children's Hospital. We went on to have a warm and supportive relationship that was never uncomfortable or brisk. As a side note, I found this doctor by looking at the Oakland Children's Hospital website under pediatric neurology and chose this particular doctor because he had good credentials and wrote an impassioned and moving explanation of why he chose to be a pediatric neurologist. This specialist, in consultation with his graduate students and colleagues, concluded that an epilepsy diagnosis was unfounded, no medication was indicated, and importantly, he spent a lot of time going through his reasoning with me and patiently answering my questions.

When you sit in the office of these providers you are incredibly vulnerable. They are passing judgment on your child while you sit helplessly and watch. You are powerless, with two important exceptions. If things seem wrong or uncomfortable for any reason, you can:

1. Demand that you and your child be better treated
2. Get up, walk out the door, and not come back

You should not suffer with any specialist, doctor, or provider who does not feel right, no matter how famous they may be. There is always someone else.

Sometimes specialists, like all of us, let their emotions get in the way of their work. This only happened to us once, but it left a strong and lasting impression. After a very intense psychotherapy session, my son felt that his psychiatrist had behaved badly and told him. I would have thought that adolescent psychiatrists dealt with this sort of thing all the time, so much so that how to respond would have been taught in medical school. This psychiatrist apparently missed that lecture, as he marched into the waiting room and summoned me to his office. There, in a shrill voice, clearly disturbed, he began a tirade on the topic of how "very seriously ill" my son was and how he "needed help immediately." This last recommendation, I might note, was what he should have been getting from this psychiatrist. There was no mention of anything that passed in the session nor any reasoned account of how he came to this conclusion. The psychiatrist's comments grew increasingly agitated. When I finally managed to interrupt him long enough to ask why he thought this and to point out that none of my son's other specialists had said anything even mildly akin to this, he ignored me. As the situation became increasingly uncomfortable, I turned to my son and with the calmest voice I could muster said, "I think we should go now." We walked swiftly out of the office, with the psychiatrist, increasingly agitated, yelling after us. I eventually came to a cordial reconciliation with this physician, but my son to this day has not.

I limit our exposure to renowned but otherwise intolerable specialists to a single visit, from which I might gain a useful theory, or idea, or referral. Ongoing care requires a partnership between you, your child's specialists, and your child. I have fortunately seen only a handful of doctors who made me feel like a brainless idiot barely worth their time. Part of being a good medical provider entails communicating in an open and thoughtful manner. You should feel treated as an intelligent and sentient adult who is part of a team working together to help your child. You should be able to get good information that moves your thinking about your child forward. You are an essential part of making any intervention work and you should feel respected and well treated by all providers and specialists involved.

V. HOW NOT TO LOSE YOUR HOPE OR YOUR MIND

You hopefully now have at least an idea of what is happening, where it does and does not affect your child's development and well-being, and a strong group of specialists working with you, or at least some good referrals for doctors and therapists with whom to follow up. Depending on the seriousness of your child's issues, you now need to rethink your perspective on and emotions about your child and how best to parent them. The news that something is not ok is shocking and disturbing. Your child may not be able to do things that other children do. They may not have the gross motor skills to play team sports, or may have difficulty staying calm enough to attend birthday parties with other children. They are "different," which makes you different as well. You and your child are now separate from the mainstream in which the majority of children and their parents move and play.

Being the parent of a non-mainstream child can be isolating and dark. It is helpful and important to remember that it doesn't have to be. Humanity exists on a continuum. Which part of that continuum is "normal," or mainstream, is determined by society. If a person's behaviors are within the set of behaviors that have been deemed "normal" by their society, then that person is considered "normal." Normal behaviors, or social norms, are arbitrary and generally emerge as a way to maintain orderly social interactions in a group or society. What is non-mainstream or "abnormal" here and now might thus be mainstream in some other place or in this place at some other point in time.

Abnormal behavior is thus identified by its deviation from social norms. Over time, in the U.S., more and more behaviors have been characterized as "abnormal." For example, a child who is irritable and has temper tantrums more than three times per week now, according to the most recent version of the canonical diagnostic manual (DSM), has a disruptive mood dysregulation disorder. At a symposium on medicalization in 2009, introductory speaker Chris Lane commented, "Medicalization isn't the most eloquent noun...but it's the best one we have for describing how common emotions and traits are (now) turned into treatable conditions... To put it bluntly, this process of pathologizing has gotten out of control. It's a juggernaut that no one seems able to stop" ("On the Medicalization"). There are some benefits to this trend, such as distracted, hyperactive children increasingly diagnosed as having attention deficit hyperactivity disorder [6] instead of just being punished or written off in school. Now these children are given accommodations such as extra time on tests or a quiet space in which to work. The net effect of this medicalization, however, is that we are viewing our children through a microscope of ever-finer resolution. What was once idiosyncrasy is now often deemed pathological, "special," or disordered.

As adults, many of us could be viewed as being "special" or non-mainstream on one or another dimensions ourselves. You have probably come across the list of accomplished adults who struggled with developmental issues and abnormal behaviors and disorders as children: Steven Spielberg, Albert Einstein, David Boies, and Quentin Tarantino to name a few. As adults, most of us have maneuvered ourselves into positions in which we can function well or at least pretty well. Being non-mainstream can, in the right circumstances, be an asset for your child. Being non-mainstream means that your child's mind and/or body operate in a manner that is not well understood and does not conform to accepted standards of how we are supposed to be. This is the definition of what it is to be creative or to operate "outside the box." Granted, not all non- mainstream

---

6. Children with attention deficit hyperactivity disorder (ADHD) have difficulty mustering attention for subjects not of interest and often are hyperactive and impulsive. Attention deficit disorder (ADD) is the antiquated name for the same condition.

children are creative in a useful and interesting way. Your child may not fit under this heading, but it is worth considering that not following society's conventional norms and standards can result in new, interesting, and innovative work and thought, both now and later in life. Our standards and norms are arbitrary and not necessarily predictive of what a child's life will be like when they are an adult. Standards give us a yardstick against which to determine if, at this point in time, a child needs extra help beyond standard parenting and schooling to thrive. When a child consistently does not meet a standard they are deemed to have an "issue," are often put under a diagnostic category, and the appropriate therapies and interventions are recommended. This diagnostic labeling gives specialists a common language but also potentially narrows and limits their thinking. I have found that the most helpful doctors and therapists did not dwell on what should be, or labor over diagnostic labels. Instead, they looked at this murky world almost from moment to moment, noting the interventions and supports that were needed now, but not being overly predictive about what could happen later. This at first was maddening, as I wanted clear, well-defined answers. What I usually got was, "we just don't know." From the pediatricians wrapped in green scrubs and masks in the neonatal ward to the various specialists and therapists along the way, no one has had answers. Eventually I came to realize that there are none, or if they exist, they are usually inaccurate or incomplete. I was told by a physical therapist, for example, that my son would have difficulty learning to write. His writing turned out to be fine, and he went on to write with the other children in his class. We were told after my son's birth that his dropped right wrist might never be ok, compromising his ability to use his right arm. After physical therapy for four months, his wrist was fine. This was a common experience, a prediction of doom generally turned out not to be doom at all. You will come to understand that for most physicians and specialists, in most of the circumstances you will encounter, there is too much uncertainty in this world of non-mainstream children to make predictions and prognoses with much confidence. Years ago, I asked a world-renowned pediatric neurologist at UCSF, (University of California San

Francisco Medical Center), what the possible range of outcomes might be for my newborn son, who had just come through a traumatic birth. He answered, "well, he could live or he could die." Although this answer bewildered and irritated me at the time, I eventually came to realize that he was saying the future was a vast unknown. The difference with a non-mainstream child is that the range of possibilities is much greater and more terrifying at its extremes. There are both potentially devastating disabilities at one end and also possibly brilliant and creative acts at the other. It is largely uncharted territory and your job is to find a stable equilibrium for yourself, your child, and your family, amidst all this uncertainty. Notwithstanding the advances of modern medicine, developmental problems and issues in children are not well understood.

At some point I realized that my pursuit of clarity and prediction about the future was also in part a need to manage my own expectations. Should I gird myself for a world of compromises and never ending concerns, or should I be waiting in anxious anticipation for my child's great step into the mainstream as a creative and brilliant presence? Was my child going to be unable to participate in the standard rituals of American childhood, or would he be able to move ahead, successfully making his own path? For me, this ambiguity was one of the most difficult aspects of having a child outside the mainstream. It often became an exercise in disciplining my emotions. I had to both hold in check any plans and expectations I might have had, while at the same time holding all outcomes as a possibility. I had to hold onto the possibility of having our family live in a foreign country, something I had always wanted to do, while also making sure that I knew which San Francisco special needs schools might work for us, should we need one in the future. Along the way there were always the comforting anecdotes. A developmental pediatrician once told me that he would wager a good portion of the humanities faculty at Harvard had some form of Asperger's syndrome, a high functioning form of autism. If he is right, those people as children today would have had stressed and worried parents laboring with the specter that their child might never move out of the autistic spectrum to function successfully and independently.

One of my favorite distractions at parties is to peruse the room imagining the catalog of disorders I might assign to the guests around me. The hugely successful academic and consultant friend who is reluctant to make eye contact, or the wife of a colleague who cannot stop anxiously babbling would both fit nicely into diagnostic categories. It is actually not very hard to put a diagnosis on just about everyone. What keeps us all from having a classifiable disorder is just a question of threshold, classification, and timing. Where the boundary lies between health and disorder is usually arbitrary. Our non-mainstream children are perceived as being "not normal" but as adults, if they are able to find their way into something they love and do well, they could be just fine. There is an adage a psychologist once told me years ago that to this day I still remember and find comforting; the most interesting adults were always the most difficult and problematic children.

So, you may be raising a math genius, or a future filmmaker, or a playwright, or a humanities professor at an Ivy League school. Your child's thinking and behavior is different and, for now, is deemed "disordered," or "delayed," or in some other way not mainstream or appropriate for their age. This means that you will have to be ready to respond to both the successes and the failures. This is not all that different from what any parent must do, except the extremes are much greater. You will have to let yourself enjoy the days when teachers say your child is gifted and their work is brilliant and unlike anything they have ever seen. You will also have to stay calm when you receive calls from your child's school telling you that they have pinched someone in an inappropriate place, or are disruptive in class, or that a behavior is so outrageous and inappropriate that it is outside the boundaries of anything the school has ever seen. There was a period of time in which I received a call from the Head of my son's Upper School nearly every day and sometimes multiple times a day. The Head once told me that the most interesting conversation he had ever had at the school, bar none, was with my son. The Head called another day about an incident in which complicated payoffs had been made to children in a popular social clique so that they would fight with one another and be suspended. Orchestrated by my son, using his Christmas and birthday money, complete with detailed schematics, accounting, and notes on the outcome for future reference. This was a remarkable feat from a child who supposedly had executive function weaknesses. During this period of time I would shudder every time my cellphone rang. One day my son would be sent home or be close to being suspended and the next he would be impressing people with his humanity and creativity, or be accelerated several grades forward into an advanced writing class. The highs are ecstatic and the lows can be very low and very depressing. You have to be there through all of it. You have to chart a stable course, integrating what you see and hear, and evaluating each new incident as either further evidence in support of your thinking, or as a reason to rethink your hypothesis about where your child's weaknesses lay, how your child's functioning is affected, and what you should be doing to help. Every interaction and behavior that falls outside your understanding is new information that you need to pursue and eventually incorporate into your thinking. For example, seeing your child operate well in a playgroup could mean that they can in fact read social clues, despite what their therapists may have told you or the diagnosis they are carrying. If this is true, you may be able to stop the therapy that addresses this weakness. You may also be able to eliminate both a diagnostic label hanging over your child and your trepidation every time your child enters a new play situation. There is then also the question of whether this is unique to this particular situation and what that is telling you about your child. All this is information that you will have to try to understand. When my son was in his last years of primary school we learned that he was extremely anxious. This knowledge made his hyperactive behavior, attention deficit, and social isolation more understandable. The more anxious he became, the more hyperactive his behavior, and the less he could attend to what was happening around him. The complex of his issues began to form a coherent story and make sense.

Once your child is deemed non-mainstream, based on observation, testing, and evaluations, they will be grouped in medical providers' minds, either under a diagnosis and/or with a set of potential deficits. These deficits may or may not be a part of your child's problem, and you will have to ferret out what is and is not applicable to your child. You should be constantly testing your operating hypotheses as to what your child's strengths and weaknesses are, how they fit into your current thinking, and how to best support them. After being diagnosed as autistic, a girl we knew was not expected to interact well or be able to play with peers. [7] Her playground time was then eliminated in favor of speech therapy. In fact, she was able to play well with peers. When her mother realized this, she put the girl back on the playground, got a second opinion, and eventually her daughter was diagnosed not as autistic, but as having a non-verbal learning disorder, a condition with a much more optimistic prognosis.

Whoever it is you are raising, you still have to learn to negotiate this new world without losing yourself in the myriad of details you now have to hold in mind. A non-mainstream child is more work on almost every dimension. They might not be as autonomous and independent as their peers, due to an attention deficit, some anxiety condition, or autistic spectrum issue. Getting dressed in the morning may be a trial, remembering assignments and appointments may be hard, they may not easily make friends. They probably will need to be driven to multiple therapies and appointments. You will have to explain to teachers, childcare providers, other parents, and people at home and around you that your child needs certain special accommodations, and then explain what those accommodations are. You are the point person for coordinating everything. I often found myself frenzied and tense. At times I felt that I had lost my ability to hold a normal conversation and just be present with family and friends in real time. I was forever observing or rushing off to appointments and meetings to try to understand some new and puzzling aspect of my son's behavior. I would advise you to look for ways to get as much help as you can and to hand off the tasks that you can comfortably delegate.

---

7. Children with autism have difficulty processing emotions and interpreting social cues. As a result, they often find it difficult to interact with others.

Use grandparents, siblings, friends, and other relatives as much as possible and give them whatever enticements they need to continue helping. One woman I knew had her sister move in with her. In trade for helping with the children, the sister got free room and board. I used to put advertisements for help on bulletin boards at the local psychology and therapy programs. This yielded some great people who had both knowledge of unusual child development, and a lot of sensitivity and patience. They usually did not want an excessive hourly rate as well. Once I found someone I liked, I would then do everything possible to make their work situation with me the best it could be. Having a non-mainstream child is at times exhausting, with help it will still be exhausting, but maybe a little less so.

Something I never did and should have done was to seek out other parents with non-mainstream children. There are support groups, blogs, events, and meetings that are easy to find online. I recommend that you participate in these social groups for several reasons. First, it is often difficult to find playmates for a non-mainstream child and these groups are a source of other families with children who can potentially be playmates. It is also helpful to have kindred spirits with whom you do not have to explain your child and what they are doing and feeling. There is also a lot of practical wisdom to be gained from others in a similar situation. For example, referrals for good specialists, shopkeepers to avoid because they have no patience for frenetic ADHD children, cafes that offer gluten and dairy-free snacks, and so on. These groups are also a potential source of emotional support, which is essential. I am fortunate in having a devoted and resourceful mother and several dear friends who pretty much went through every trying moment with me. This was essential to my emotional survival.

It is important also to notice your child's strengths and to look for ways and situations in which they can be successful. No matter what their developmental issues are, there will be areas in which your child functions well and may even excel. Find the activities that engage your child's areas of strength. Join playgroups, camps, classes, and/or whatever else is available that is interesting to your child. We knew an autistic boy who was a remarkable artist. His parents were forever finding places where he could draw and paint and then exhibit his work. It was a huge source of pride for him to see his work on the walls of his school and elsewhere.

Your child's limitations also have to be accommodated. Sometimes structural changes can be helpful. Asking a friend to come over or hiring a really patient childcare person to be there after dinner when your exhausted husband does not have the patience to deal with your obsessive compulsive (OCD) child, and you are exhausted as well, can help a lot. I recommend that you try to anticipate points of conflict and manage your child's life and your life to eliminate as many of these as you can. This might mean, for example, keeping a supply of extra shirts with you so that when your anxious child finishes chewing on the one they are wearing, you can pull out another and quickly have them change instead of nagging at them to stop chewing. Buying shoes with Velcro closures because your child does not have the fine motor skills to tie shoelaces is another example. You are operating on another timetable with a non-mainstream child. Unlike mainstream children, for whom there are elaborate developmental milestones and expectations by age, no one can tell you what your child's timetable will be. If you can eliminate potential problems and conflicts, I strongly urge you to do so. Sometimes you may need to persevere through a problem for therapeutic reasons. Use your child's specialists as a guide to when this is the case. For everything else that you can structure or plan your way out of to avoid conflicts, you should do so.

It is important to pull yourself out of your child's world on a regular basis. You will be grappling with these issues for many years and you must keep yourself physically and emotionally strong. Having something into which you can immerse yourself outside the world of your child is essential. It doesn't matter what it is, as long as it captures your interest and pulls you out of your child's world. The feeling that I could not leave my child for any length of time was always present for me. I did not get away often enough, and our family suffered as a result. A trip to South Africa once taught me this invaluable and obvious lesson. My son, then an infant, for some unknown reason would not sleep, leaving me close to exhaustion. I finally let dear friends convince me that they should babysit him overnight, so that I might get some sleep. After reluctantly agreeing, I later realized that this was one of the best decisions I had ever made. My son spent time in Hermanus, on the beach with our friends and playing in a house on beautiful Walker Bay, and I felt as if I had been reborn. A valuable lesson learned.

Finally, and most importantly, to feel good about what you are doing you must make sure that you see your child as a unique individual. It is easy to get lost in the recommendations, theories, details, and logistics, and to forget that your child is a sensitive impressionable person and not just a patient under a microscope. Your child still has the needs of any other child. They are still moving through the various phases of development, learning, and experiencing the world with ever-greater understanding and knowledge. Whatever your child's issue, disorder, or delay, you should think of it as sitting between the world and your child. Your child is still there underneath, maybe obscured somewhat, or a lot. No matter how frazzled you get they still need your unconditional love, encouragement, and patience. They also need space in their life to just be a child, outside the doctor or therapist's office. It is easy to become impatient, demanding, and short-tempered. It is easy to let your world and your child's world telescope down to the seemingly endless series of appointments and corrections. When your child does not listen, or needs yet another reminder, or forgets what they should be doing, or leaves their homework behind, or whatever, it is important to find the space in your own mind to respond in a fair and gentle way. To a large extent, your child will react to and behave in the way in which you think of and treat them. We once went through an awful period in which my son, then an adolescent, was angry, rebellious, and basically intolerable. We were beside ourselves and truly clueless as to what to do and how to respond. None of the advice in books or anything our therapists recommended helped. Finally, it dawned on me that if I treated my son as the sweet, humane person he used to be and I believed he still was somewhere inside, he might respond as such. And he did. Finding the patience in myself to be kind eventually elicited the same in my son. Being positive about and confident in your child will make it much easier for them to feel good about themselves, develop self-confidence, and hopefully behave in at least a moderately cooperative manner. If you believe in them, it makes it much easier for them to believe in themselves. I was always great at organizing and planning things, but struggled to find the space to be calm, patient and encouraging. It is really easy to feel like an efficient shrew. The extent to which you can avoid this will be directly proportional to how good you will feel about yourself and your parenting.

VI. VIEWING IT ALL IN THE LARGER CONTEXT OF LIFE

We all have illusions and hopes for our children, whether we allow ourselves to be explicitly aware of them or not. Hearing that your child has "a problem" that might prevent them from someday fully realizing some innate potential or vision you might have had for them is devastating. You must remember, however, that very few of us have realized our full potential. That if we have even come close, it is rarely in the manner that we or others imagined. What is considered abnormal in a child often is viewed as eccentric in an adult. Granted there are real, lasting, and devastating childhood disabilities. Short of these, however, there is a vast range of abilities that can work successfully in adult life. Once our children are out of high school and are able to specialize, they can focus on their areas of strength. If they can't do math due to some visual spatial issue, they can attend a college without math requirements and never have to do math again beyond the occasional arithmetic. If they are dyslexic but have an aptitude for math and science, they can go to a technically oriented university. Very few of us are brilliant and for those of us who are, our talents rarely extend across all areas of life. At a particular graduate school on the East Coast, I learned that people can have near to or genius level intelligence in one area and be close to hopeless in other areas. The examples are many. There was the computer genius who could barely string a set of words together into a full sentence. A math prodigy unable to focus on the present repeatedly turned up in class dressed in his pajamas. A successful electronics inventor and entrepreneur was so shy that he was unable to make eye contact or ask for even the most basic things, like food in the cafeteria line. As long as these people stayed in or around their areas of strength, they were fine. If they had been children now, many of them would certainly have been deemed "special" or non-mainstream. There is a lot of room to be a non-mainstream child and still live a very happy, successful, and rewarding life. This is worth remembering as the barrage of diagnoses and recommendations for interventions come raining down on you. Children are measured and judged across all areas of their function when they are young. Once they specialize in what they like and can do well, then things become much easier. Until then it is a struggle and the crux of the struggle is school. School is where the confluence of our society's expectations and conventions come crashing down on the backs of non-mainstream children. They are expected to sit quietly, pay attention, remember a myriad of details and instructions, manage their frustrations and emotions in a socially appropriate way, and stay composed through it all. The artistic child has to trudge through math and science. The dyspraxic child has to participate in physical education. [8] The child with a short-term memory deficit has to struggle with a foreign language. A not insignificant number of non-mainstream children will never be well equipped to operate successfully across all areas of traditional primary, middle, and high school curricula, no matter how much support they receive. School, mercifully, is not the entirety of a life. Many schools now recognize that mainstream education does not work for all children and are trying to customize their curricula where and when they can. There are schools for special needs children as well, although these are wildly expensive. [9] Hopefully someday public education will be able to provide the customized curriculum that non-mainstream children need and all children could benefit from as a standard offering.

---

8. Dyspraxia is a developmental disorder affecting motor skills. A dyspraxic child may seem clumsy and careless when in fact there is a coordination and movement weakness not a lack of attention or care.

9. If you can show that your local public school is unable to deliver the services your child needs, they are obligated by law to pay for private school tuition and programs. Consultants are available to help with this process. A number of useful online sites can be found by googling "getting public schools to pay for private school," or something similar.

In this day of increasing specialization and ever-greater access to high quality learning online, whether it makes sense for schools to try to maneuver non-mainstream children through a standardized curriculum is unclear. For non-mainstream children whose brains may not be wired in a manner that makes the standard school subjects either intrinsically understandable or readily accessible, school can be an agony. Someday, maybe, schools will have the courage to let non-mainstream children specialize early, so that the burden of doing schoolwork for which their brains are not built is eliminated, in favor of focusing on what these children can and want to do well. I am a huge proponent of liberal education, but I often wonder if it still works to the benefit of all children.

VII. MANAGING YOUR PARTNER

This chapter makes several assumptions. The first is that you, the reader, are the principal adult overseeing your child's welfare and the coordination of doctors, therapists, and interventions. The second assumption is that your partner has taken or will take a less active role, either due to temperament, professional obligations, or for some other reason. If this is not the case, then you are already miles ahead and certainly miles ahead of where I was.

Parenting a non-mainstream child is a challenge. Things you would otherwise do without thinking now require special thought, accommodation, and effort. Coordinating this with a partner can range from difficult to near impossible. My husband and I, for example, had very different notions about how to rear our non-mainstream child. Had I realized the extent to which this was true and the conflicts it would create, I would have had us in a therapist's office from the moment we left the neonatal ward at UCSF. It is really important to sit down with your partner, in a therapist's office or wherever is comfortable, and talk about your parenting philosophy and how the two of you are going to approach your child's special challenges. This is an extension of the conversations all couples have, or should have, before and after children arrive. In the case of a non-mainstream child, the stakes are much higher, the mistakes seem much more critical and momentous, and the choices and decisions become more weighty and intense. The question of when to stand firm, how strict to be, and to what extent imposing discipline in a given situation is the right thing to do is much more nuanced and difficult. You cannot be sure that your child is capable of the behaviors and thinking most children possess at the same age. If your child does not have the ability to eat toast without making a huge pile of crumbs because they are dyspraxic, for example, being a stickler about table manners and decorum is not going to work to anyone's benefit. An ongoing source of conflict in our household was the extent to which our young son was able to follow good table manners at meals. My husband was adamant that things like keeping crumbs on a plate or jam on a knife were within our son's abilities. If these tasks could be mastered, he reasoned, the discipline and attention needed for mastery could then be generalized to other areas. This is a reasonable idea but I was skeptical. There were signs that our son was dyspraxic, and even if he wasn't, it didn't seem worth the stress this created at each meal. Being too flexible, however, has its problems as well. Will your child get used to the idea that because they are "special" the rules don't apply, or will always bend for them? Will they develop, ironically, a sense of entitlement because they are outside the normal expectations for polite, well-behaved children, and always get special attention and accommodations? It is a delicate balance, which is made all the more difficult by the fact that your child is constantly changing, hence their abilities are changing, and thus your parenting expectations and demands must change as well. All this makes the coordination and consensus that are essential to good parenting extremely difficult. Particularly if you and your partner disagree as to where your child's abilities lie relative to your expectations and on the appropriate level of parenting discipline to begin with. It is an ongoing challenge that can easily build resentment.

So, how do you create common ground when you and your partner have differing views on your child and how to parent them? You must start from a point at which you are together in your thinking and doing. This means understanding your own and then your partner's belief system about children, childhood, and parenting. For example, do you believe that children should be allowed to develop with minimal intervention? Do you believe that your child should have a say in the decision-making and the setting of boundaries? Or are you more authoritarian, setting rules that must be followed or a punishment results? How you will react to your child's inevitable infringement of your boundaries and eschewing of your values is essential to understand. There is a wide continuum. You must understand explicitly where each of you is on this continuum, then try to agree on a place somewhere in between where you can be together. You will have to find a position that is comfortable for both of you and that you both agree to and will follow. In our case, our views of childhood were very different. One of us saw childhood as a time for open and free exploration. The other saw it as more of an ongoing education in the values, discipline, and knowledge necessary to be a humane and well-educated person. Each of these positions is valuable, but each has very different implications for parenting. Together, these points of view lie in direct contrast. If you can remember that multiple points of view can be valuable, and integrating these into a coherent whole is powerful, hopefully that will lead to a middle ground that is acceptable to each of you. Your therapists and psychiatrist can have important input to this conversation but in the end each of you as a parent, living with your child, will have to believe in what you are doing. This should be a partnership. Your aim is to get to a point from which each of you believes that you are working together towards common and mutually agreed upon goals.

Couples often jump into parenting without these conversations. As a result, disaster can ensue. When your parenting style is unclear, it is both destructive to your relationship and can cause confusion for your child, who may already be having difficulty making sense of the world due to their developmental issues. If you have very different points of view it can be really hard or close to impossible to find middle ground. It may require the help of a therapist or some other intermediary. You do not want one perspective to dominate and the other not to be heard. This is a formula for resentment and worse.

In addition to finding a common ground in your parenting style, it is important that you both feel engaged and involved with your child's life. Given that your non-mainstream child will take up such a large portion of your common time, staying connected as a couple is much easier if you are both directly involved with your child. Keeping up with what is happening is essential to this end. For example, each of you should go to at least the initial therapist and doctor appointments to meet these people and then, if possible, also go to subsequent progress meetings to keep up with what is happening. Being together at important meetings creates a sense of partnership and hopefully collective agreement or collective disagreement about what the provider is recommending. It also has the added benefit of giving you two interpretations of what was said in a given meeting. It is not enough for one parent to go to the meetings and then brief the other, no matter how consumed with commitments the other may be. Although this might seem efficient and reasonable, it is too easy for one partner to become alienated and resentful. This inevitably happens because one person is out in the world while the other is sitting in doctor or therapist waiting rooms, or because one of you develops a closer relationship to your child while the other feels left out. It also puts one partner in a secondary position with respect to your child's upbringing and life.

Another issue is time. Finding time to do the work required to maintain a healthy rapport with your partner is difficult. When you have a child, it is yet more difficult. When you have a non-mainstream child, it is more difficult still. Finding time to be together apart from your child and their issues is a challenge. With a non-mainstream child, the available free time is less and the parenting questions and required activities are more, both in frequency and complexity. Solutions to this problem are the obvious ones. If you can get away on a regular basis for one or more evenings or weekends, that helps. It is hard though not to carry your concerns about your child to these outings, which can become de facto therapy sessions or progress reviews. You must fight this inclination. The time for therapy or for progress reviews is in the offices of your child's providers. Time together completely outside your child's world is essential, even if it is just a walk up the fire road. For every couple it will be different, but carving out the psychological space that every relationship needs is crucial. It is something to be constantly aware of and working towards.

Mainstream children create stress and non-mainstream children create even more stress. In my experience, when we are stressed we tend to retreat to what is familiar and comfortable. In our case, this meant gravitating to the parenting styles we each grew up with, which were polar opposites and exaggerations of our belief systems today. One of us became authoritarian, making discipline, rules, and the enforcement of rules paramount. The other took a much more flexible approach in which understanding why something happened was paramount and the appropriate reaction was flexible, depending upon the circumstances. If you can recognize the place to which each of you goes when stressed and where each of your extreme parenting places is, then you have a chance at stopping yourselves from going there. Awareness can go a long way towards change, or at least can mitigate behavior. At a minimum, it will make understanding after the fact easier.

In the end, if you are to survive happily, you will somehow have to find common ground. How you do this and what it will be depends on you, but working as a team towards the common goal of helping support your child, while also creating a life that is fulfilling to you both, is the essential task. It is easy to forget this, or assume it is happening when it isn't. The scenario of one partner earning the income to pay your large therapy bills and the other staying at home managing your child's life is particularly vulnerable. You will likely not have or not often have the heart-warming moments that commonly hold partners together. Your child will often be a source of stress and conflict, not the warmth that can dissipate tension and make it all feel worth the trouble. It is easy to become isolated and resentful. You must actively work to prevent this resentment from occurring and address it when it does. The stories of couples splitting up after parenting a non-mainstream child, sadly, are all too many.

VIII. HOW TO CREATE A REASONABLE HOME LIFE

Certain former associates and friends of mine will smile at this chapter title, as I did not succeed in creating a reasonable home life at a time when we desperately needed one. With the value of hindsight, however, I can see that this is possible. It takes many acts of will and discipline against values and beliefs that I, and probably you, hold in common. The first of these is the desire to see our children succeed by the normal measures and achievements of our society. Non-mainstream children will not do this in the ways we can imagine, at least not most of the time. They will be operating on their own timetable, with their own version of the milestones on the developmental charts. The standard achievements and benchmarks of childhood and adolescent life will elude them in many cases. They will likely not do the things they are supposed to do, at least not when they are supposed to do them. This may mean that these milestones and achievements don't come at all, or come later, or come in some completely different order or form. Crawling and walking may be delayed, speech may be late, coordination may be off, and handwriting messy and potentially never up to standard. These are not catastrophic departures by any means, but as your child grows their variations on the standard childhood developmental model often become more concerning. School will likely be problematic, friendships may be difficult, attention may be and often is an issue. The list goes on and on.

There are in my observation two principal parental approaches to these departures from the path of "normal" childhood development. Either you fight to keep your child on or as close to the mainstream as possible, or you let your child float off the mainstream into an unknown world with no clear milestones and no really well understood path. The first path is crazy making and stressful, the second anxiety provoking and potentially terrifying. Either way you are faced with a situation that is difficult to manage in a manner that makes for a serene and healthy home-life. In some cases you won't have a choice. Your child's issues may be significant enough to make being in the mainstream not possible or even conceivable. Or your child's issues may be mild enough to make the mainstream an obvious and clearly appropriate choice. Many non-mainstream children, however, fall somewhere between these two extremes. You then have to figure out which path is best for them, for you, and for your family. It is this large grey zone that I want to speak about in this chapter.

The mainstream is a place where most of us would like our children to be, or at least be able to be. We would like our children to attend a local school, play with friends, and do what children generally do when they are happy and thriving. The decision to try to stay in the mainstream is a cost-benefit decision. What price do you have to pay and are you willing to pay, and to have your family pay, must be measured against how much benefit your non-mainstream child will get in return. Staying in the mainstream with a non-mainstream child is likely to mean nightly homework sessions with you or someone else, (the latter is highly recommended if you can manage it), because your child is not able to complete their homework alone. Non-mainstream children often have executive function issues resulting in poor organizational ability. They will need help deciding when things should be done, what order to do them in, when they need to be someplace, and how to think about all this as a coherent, sequenced whole. Play dates and making friends can be a problem, as your child will be meeting children without significant issues who may not want to play with them because they are different. Your child's success on this path will depend on the severity and nature of their issues, their determination to succeed, and on the extent to which you and your family can be supportive and handle the ensuing stress and conflict. There will be fights about doing homework, finishing assignments, getting dressed, being ready for the next new thing, and generally getting things done when required. Your child will be thrown together with children, teachers and parents who may not understand them and may not be sympathetic or accommodating. Your child will be in a peer group with children who most likely are at higher levels of function in some or many areas. This path can be stressful for everyone in the family, most of all for your non-mainstream child. This path can also be a recipe for disaster and takes lots of vigilance, constant reevaluation, and huge amounts of patience.

The advantages of the mainstream path are many. Your child will be modeling their behavior on developmentally mainstream children. The language your child hears and on which they model their speech will most likely be age appropriate or above. Your child will be getting a mainstream curriculum at school, maybe even an enriched curriculum, which is well understood by teachers, parents, and the school. There is also the hope that if you support your child along this path, they will eventually transition to doing it themselves and the supports and stress would then fall away.

On the negative side, you will be interacting with parents of mainstream children and will have to explain the more unusual aspects of your child's behavior. If not able to follow or keep up with the terms of play, your child may be made to feel like an outcast, an other, or "weird" by peers. Your child may at times be the only child in the class who needs help, differentiating them from the other students. There are no guarantees that these things won't happen on the non-mainstream path but on that path there are more children who are "different" and hopefully this creates a more flexible set of expectations for performance and social conduct. In the mainstream, in school and elsewhere, teachers and adults without training in special needs may become impatient, frustrated, and act badly toward your child. Classmates, detecting that something is different, may be cruel and mean. Being in an environment where expectations may be too demanding for your child can be exhausting, potentially depressing, and demoralizing. This last consideration should be at the top of your hierarchy of questions about this path. The mainstream is not a healthy place for all children. The mainstream will require you to be actively and constantly vigilant, monitoring your child's environment to make sure they are not being pushed too hard, or mistreated, or misunderstood.

You will be spending a lot of time with your child and on issues concerning your child, to the possible neglect of other members of your family. The whole household can, if you are not careful, begin to revolve around your non-mainstream child and the accommodations needed to keep them "on-track," potentially creating resentment in your partner and your other children, if any. You will be performing a balancing act between your child's abilities and the expectations of the mainstream world around them. You will be the translator between these worlds. To be successful, you will have to insure that both sides are happy. If this sounds exhausting, rest assured it is.

If you choose to let your child float off the mainstream, the stress on you, your child, and your family will be greatly reduced. Your child will be in a special school or program in which expectations for organization, behavior, homework, and general performance and demeanor will be more flexible. The families and children with whom you and your child interact will be inhabitants of this non-mainstream world as well. Thus the required translation should be less. Most people will have practice in making accommodations and hopefully will have the patience to do so graciously, in a manner that is positive and supportive for your child. Classroom expectations will be more lenient and flexible. Everyone will assume from the start that there are issues that need to be accommodated and addressed. This may sound like a godsend, and in many ways it is, but there are as always additional considerations. Your child will be in a class and school in which the other children have some sort of developmental issue or problem. As a result, your child's peers and peer role models will be different and unusual, possibly in a way that is not positive. Behaviors will almost certainly be more extreme and problematic, as children struggling with developmental issues are trying to make sense of and function in a world that is more frustrating and difficult to manage.

In this world, however, your child will hopefully not be an outsider. There are no guarantees, and children with developmental issues can be mean and cruel as well, but there is a good chance this world will be more benign. If you choose the non-mainstream path, you are putting your child in a group of available peers that might not be as high-functioning as you would hope. What is interesting and challenging about this choice is that you cannot know if this group includes the next Einstein, or Bill Gates, or the nonverbal autistic child down the street who will always be challenged and struggling. You cannot know who these children ultimately will be, what their capabilities really are, and thus what their impact on your child will be. All you can know is that for now their development is problematic for some reason and your child is in there with them, for better and for worse. This is the fundamental difficulty with the non-mainstream path. It is unknown, its inhabitants are not well understood, and its milestones are not well defined. It is a murky unconventional place, which can be very scary. If modern medicine was able to completely understand our children, then this path would be ideal. But this is not the case today. No one really knows what is going on within non-mainstream children, what they will become, and what they really need, in a refined sense. By putting your child on this path you are taking a huge risk, as nothing here is well known or well understood, and some parts of this path may not be very desirable.

The non-mainstream path should be much less stressful for you and your family if you can truly embrace it, quell your fears as to where it will lead, and just let your child unfold. This was more than I could do at the time I was faced with this choice. I opted to try to stay in the mainstream. For years our family life was stressed as a result. My husband used to say he was afraid to come home at the end of the work day for fear that he would walk into the middle of some huge argument about homework. I spent hours helping with schoolwork and was distracted and exhausted for much of that time. There were happy moments, but my son was isolated and different from the other children for much of his primary school career. He was though in a place where the people around him did not lower their expectations for what he could do or who he was. He was not, as a therapist once warned, "warehoused" as special needs children often are. Nor was he written off as "special." We paid a very high price to stay in the mainstream. Whether it was worth it is something I will never know but often wonder about.

IX. THINGS THAT CAN HELP

Routine is at the top of almost every therapist's recommendation list. Make daily life activities repetitive and familiar. Create a routine or schedule, hopefully one that works, and stay with it. Our morning routine never wavered: get up, put on clothes that had been carefully laid out on the floor the night before, come upstairs for breakfast, after breakfast go to the upstairs bathroom for washing (fewer distractions), grab the backpack carefully packed the night before, and finally get in the car to go to school. Non-mainstream children often have trouble negotiating their way through novel situations and environments and this is one of the common antidotes. One boy we knew was petrified of airplanes until his therapist suggested they create a routine for going to the airport and getting on an airplane. At home they recreated the security lines, took off their shoes, put things into bins, imagined the walkway onto the plane, and once inside the plane (a large box), buckled up seat belts the therapist had found somewhere, and imagined they were off. After many rounds of practice, the boy was able to take his next airplane trip without problem. Some families get permission to come to school before it is in session so that they can walk their child through the activities that will happen during the day. This creates a familiar routine. It is especially helpful if your child is starting at a new school, as the physical layout will be unfamiliar and potentially confusing and scary. You are trying to take as much uncertainty out of your child's life as possible. I have always thought of this recommendation as creating a neutral shell in which your child can operate, hopefully with fewer distractions and less stress. It is interesting that therapists want to see non-mainstream children, who are often intensely creative, living lives that are systematic and routine, exactly the opposite of what I would have thought they needed. The operating hypothesis, however, is that if you can eliminate uncertainty, which then reduces stress, your child has more space to work on their issues, be creative, and focus on their areas of strength and interest. You are creating a framework within which your child can operate comfortably. Eventually your child will have to transition to a more realistic world. For now, you are limiting the variables they have to negotiate so that they can have a more benign environment in which to learn and be.

Another important suggestion is to modify the world in which your child operates. You want to remove as many external sources of conflict and confusion as you can. If your child is profoundly distracted, for example, don't offer him five choices, offer two. If your child is not able to tie or buckle his shoes, buy shoes with Velcro closures. When therapy becomes tedious, offer the option of going to a favorite bakery afterwards. You are trying to anticipate and then engineer your way out of potential issues and conflicts as much as you can.

It is also important to create space for other members of your family, particularly your partner. When friends or family members were visiting I always asked them for at least one night of babysitting. This created an adult space in which my husband and I could go out or at least be alone together. In a nearby neighborhood a group of friends would get together and trade off having one couple babysit each week, so the other adults could have an evening or daytime alone with a partner or another child. You somehow must learn to allocate your time and energy in a manner that allows you to be accessible to the people you care about. You must find a way to be accessible to yourself as well. This requires a lot of creativity. Taking a Zen approach can at times be helpful. If you are able to be intensely present in each moment, such that whatever is happening and/or whomever you are with has your complete and undivided attention, you may be able to make up in intensity what you cannot give in time. I was rarely able to do this and spent most of my time parallel processing. I scheduled appointments in my head while playing games. I plotted out next week's schedule while listening to piano concerts. The end result was to experience nothing fully or completely, which often left me and those close to me frustrated and annoyed.

Trips can help, even short day trips. Getting away as a

family or alone provides an opportunity to get out from under the expectations and demands weighing on you. We tried to take at least one long and then two or three shorter trips at roughly the same time each year. This provided a much needed break that we could count on and look forward to. Our trips were some of our happiest times together as a family. There were no therapists, no homework, no stress about doing things differently from the way they should be done, no pressure to be someplace at a set time. It was glorious. Interestingly my son, who often struggled to sit still, had no problem sitting on twelve-hour plane flights or standing in eternally long customs lines. I am sure there is some explanation for this. Maybe awareness that our days were open ended and free, without stress or obligation?

What about you? Despite being at the bottom of the hierarchy, you too have needs. Obvious answers are exercise, meditation, and getting away, even if it is just to take your current book down the hill to a local cafe. This will not change the fact that you are a limited resource with seemingly unlimited demands placed on you. There is no easy answer beyond trying to find small windows of time for the things and people you care about and letting go of everything that is not essential in that moment.

In the end, what helped me the most was perspective. Being able to push myself beyond my own rigid constraints. Letting go of what should be in favor of the open-ended place of what was now, floating in the unknown, unattached to anything I knew or ever thought I wanted. In the moments when I was able do this, I was the happiest.

X. PARENTING A NON-MAINSTREAM CHILD

Parenting well is difficult, challenging, and humbling. No matter who you are or how prestigious your position in life may be, at some point you will be made to feel like a shallow nitwit. Parenting a non-mainstream child adds yet another layer of complexity to an already challenging job. In large part this is because you often cannot really understand which aspects of your child's behavior are truly within their control, and hence amenable to your interventions and discipline. The standard practice of penalty and reward thus becomes difficult to implement fairly and to a useful end. The standard expectations for behavior often must be revised. You will likely have to alter your ideas as to where your child can comfortably fit and what they can comfortably do. You cannot, for example, expect a child with an attention deficit disorder to listen attentively during a math session if math is not interesting to him. A child with a sensory disorder will not be able to stay calm and composed amongst other children at a loud and chaotic birthday party. [10] Your child may not be able to play catch due to gross motor issues or participate in the team sports that can tie communities and families together. You will need to work closely with your doctors and therapists and be extremely observant to understand what is and what is not reasonably within your child's ability and control. Anything you believe they can control is fair game for parental discipline and expectation. You also must remember, however, that even if your child can control a given behavior, it still may be much

---

10. A sensory processing disorder is a condition in which sensory signals entering the brain are not interpreted or organized correctly. This makes it difficult to act on information taken in by the senses. As a result, children with sensory processing disorders often feel overwhelmed.

harder for them than for a mainstream child. For example, an ADHD child may be capable of sitting through an entire Fado concert, but it takes a lot more energy and discipline for them than it would for a mainstream child. Hence it is much more tiring and difficult. I spent many a concert and theater performance walking around outside in the hall with my son because he could not sit still for long periods of time.

There is also the challenge of creating a balance between giving your child space and intervening to help them. Non-mainstream children need a lot of help and for some children it may feel like every aspect of their behavior needs a correction of one sort or another all the time. Non-mainstream children will, like any children, need time in which to be alone, have their own space, and be themselves without correction or intervention. It is easy to forget that you cannot be intervening every moment, even when they are doing things that grate on you and don't even come close to meeting your expectations. It helps if you can create a special space that is safe and contains lots of constructive things with which your child can play and explore. This space ideally should be organized to create as little conflict as possible. For example, if you have a child with a sensory disorder, you probably don't want to surround them with a lot of strong smells or toys that make loud noises. A child with fine motor deficits might have lots of building toys, but carefully chosen to be large enough to avoid frustration. Ideally, you would like to surround your child with activities that will help strengthen their weaknesses and promote their interests without you having to be there to intervene.

It is also important to remember that your child is continuing to grow and develop like any other child. You may not see this clearly, as your child's issues may obscure it, but you will still need to adjust your parenting to be in synch with your child's growing developmental maturity. Non-mainstream children, like all children, will need increasing autonomy and will want to feel increasing agency over their world as they grow and develop. Depending on your child's issues, you may have to be creative in figuring out how this can happen while still keeping them safe.

Parents of non-mainstream children often find it difficult

to relate to and bond with their child in the ways that most parents do. You may have a child who doesn't like to be hugged due to a sensory disorder, or a child who doesn't speak because of an expressive language disorder or emotional problem, or a child who never stops moving due to hyperactivity. You may not be able to have the standard parent to child conversations or quiet bedtime reading together. You may not be able to teach them things through discussion and example. The rituals that typically strengthen the bond between child and parent may not be present in a form that you recognize. It is still possible to create rituals, but it will take some work and ingenuity on your part. It is your job as parent to find ways in, past the sensory disorder or hyperactivity or language deficit, or whatever the issue may be. When my son was young, he was fascinated by unusual things, such as the small plastic dividers that separate road lanes, which we came to call "bumps." Crossing the street he would stop, kneel down on his haunches and intensely study these pieces of plastic. My husband found out where these "bumps" were made and bought some. He and my son then sat on the floor together playing with the bumps, which became a sort of bonding ritual. Another example is a boy we knew who barely spoke, but who had remarkable balance and loved to walk, actually it was more like dance, on railings. The first time I saw him my impulse was to run over and steady him, but his mother stopped me. Their ritual was to drive around finding interesting railings on which this boy could walk while his mother stood nearby watching.

The bond you ultimately forge with your child may not look like anything you recognize as a connection with another human being, but if it works for you and your child then that's all that matters. Bonding is made all the more difficult by the fact that the warm moments that parents typically have with their children may not or may not often take place. And as with nearly everything else, once you have found a means by which to connect with your child it will have to change over time. This will be either because your child has grown past it or because the circumstances have changed in some important way. When our son was young, one of his favorite rituals was to chase my husband around the living room couch. After my husband tore a ligament in a skiing accident, he was no longer able to run and had to find another game through which to communicate and relate to our son. When things change it is your job as a parent to find new ways to be connected and together with your child. Therapists can be a huge help, particularly physical and occupational therapists, who are a boundless source of practical ideas and solutions.

XI. MANAGING YOUR CHILD'S SCHOOLING AND LEARNING

Finding a good school environment for a non-mainstream child is like trying to fit a square peg into a round hole. Fortunately, there are many ways to learn besides a traditional classroom and your child will have many teachers outside of school. There is a lot of "organic learning" that goes on as well. A psychologist once consoled us by explaining that the phenomenon of "organic learning" was happening all the time. This meant that our son was learning and taking in knowledge just by virtue of interacting with the world, even if he did not seem to be present and paying attention.

Finding the right school is difficult. Depending on the magnitude and nature of your child's issues, it can be really difficult. You are looking for an environment in which your child's weaknesses and strengths are well understood and will be accepted and supported. This means that there are teachers with whom your child can learn and classrooms in which they can feel comfortable. Ideally, you would also like to find a community in which your child can feel accepted, welcome, and hopefully thrive. We made the mistake, with the encouragement of our therapists, of trying to get our son into the most academically rigorous schools we could find. This seemed an obvious strategy as he is very smart. It was, however, a mistake. Starting with the most rigorous schools we believed our son could get into and working our way down to the less demanding schools did not ultimately serve him well. We pursued schools that were indeed excellent, just not excellent for our son. We reasoned that he would grow to fit in, even though the children at these schools did not seem to have developmental issues, nor did the schools seem very interested in supporting developmental issues. When we received rejection letters everywhere we trudged, depressed and disheartened, to the "second tier" schools. These schools had easier admissions criteria and as a result their populations were more varied. The schools that rejected us actually did us a favor. They forced us to rethink our strategy. We then came to see that we should have looked closely at the children in each school from the perspective of our son as he was then, not as what we hoped he would become.

I am aware of five basic routes for schooling your child: the mainstream route with accommodations, the non-mainstream route, schools that call themselves progressive and/or developmental (which fall somewhere in the middle), home schooling, and starting your own school.

Trying to get a non-mainstream child successfully through a mainstream school can be a formidable challenge. Mainstream schools often do not have the resources to support non-mainstream children. If they do have sufficient resources for special needs, the quality and range of services and the expertise of providers may be limited. These limitations are almost always economic. Non-mainstream children need more individualized attention, which means smaller classes, more teachers, more resources, and hence more cost. In the case of private or parochial schools, the resources available will flow from the vision for the school. If that vision does not include a wide range of children at the school, there will be limited resources for children with special needs. Schools with restricted admission, such as private or parochial schools, scribe a developmental window for the children they hope to admit based on the school's vision. This window is defined by a certain level of developmental ability. If a child has this ability level or higher, they fall within the window and are a viable candidate for admission. If not, then barring some special circumstance, they will be rejected. At the time we were applying to schools, a San Francisco family with a non-mainstream child and significant resources offered to staff and equip an entire special needs program at an otherwise mainstream and very selective private school. They proposed to fund an endowment for additional teachers, specialists, and resources. Their child, who was outside the school's developmental window and would otherwise not have been admitted, could then be admitted and perform successfully. This story has a nice ending. The net effect of the family's gift was not only to get their child admitted to this school but also to broaden the range of children the school could serve. The school population became more varied and children who would otherwise not have passed the admissions screen became viable candidates.

The developmental window scribed by schools that select their students, (mainly private and parochial schools but also some public), is defined by:

- Reasoning Ability and Attention
- Receptive and Expressive Language Ability
- Visual-Spatial Skills
- Fine and Gross Motor Skills
- Impulse Control
- Quality of Interactions with Peers and Adults

among other attributes. The admissions process is primarily an exercise in determining which children meet the school's targets in each area. Schools make this decision based on testing, preschool teacher recommendations, and observing the child during a school visit. The entire curriculum and experience in the school will be crafted to meet the developmental needs of children who meet or exceed these targets. The classrooms, the teachers, the activities, and the behavioral and academic expectations will all be geared to this developmental level. Schools do make mistakes. A mainstream private school could admit your child, thinking they fell inside their window when actually they didn't. When schools make this mistake, they usually try to provide additional support but often end up counseling the child out. If this happened to your child, and your child managed somehow to stay at the school, you would likely have to provide extra support or at least manage and coordinate it. This has the potential to drive you crazy. If you look at mainstream schools that have selective admissions, it is essential to figure out where the school's developmental window lies and whether your child fits inside it.

Public schools are another mainstream option. Your local public school is required by federal law to provide your child with "a free appropriate public education in the least restrictive environment appropriate to their individual needs" ("A Guide to Disability Rights Laws"). If you can show that your child's needs cannot be met by the local public schools in a "free and appropriate" manner but could be met by a particular private school or program, then your child's education at that private school or program must by law be paid by your local school district.

Within the public schools, services are stretched across many children with diverse needs. As a result, public schools are often not as effective as they might be. Again, the problem is funding. Public schools, like all schools, have limited funds to allocate across the many needs, and special needs services are expensive. A special needs curriculum requires special classroom materials, a quiet and calm setting in which children can receive individualized instruction, and teachers with special training. All this is hugely expensive, at a time when most school districts are struggling to meet the most basic needs of even their mainstream children. I have rarely met a family with a special needs child who kept their child in the public school system when they had another reasonable option. There may be public schools that serve non-mainstream children well, but the confluence of factors that makes this possible seems to be rare. We knew a couple who took the approach that their local public school was far from perfect, but the private school options weren't all that much better. As public school was free, they used the money saved on tuition to add extra programs and classes for their child. This is another approach, but again it requires a lot of management and oversight. The couple had to identify additional programs and classes, get their son there and back, and make sure everything worked successfully.

Public preschool has been an early and ongoing initiative of the Obama administration. As currently conceived, early public education in the U.S. serves four-year old to kindergarten age children, is managed state-by-state, and is far from broadly perfected. According to The National Institute for Early

Education Research's State of Preschool 2015 report, "...for the nation as a whole, access to a high-quality preschool program remained highly unequal, ...and this year's rate of progress is not enough to bring high-quality pre-K to every child any time soon" (Barnett).

Non-mainstream, or special needs schools are another option and can be extraordinarily expensive and disappointing. When they work they are amazing. Like private and parochial schools, they will have a developmental window based on their vision for the school and they will try to accept children who fall inside that window. Unlike private and parochial schools, the special needs school window is often not well defined, or is defined as any child who falls through the private and parochial school admissions process, or any child who cannot function successfully in a mainstream school environment. As with any school, there is strong pressure to admit enough children to fill the available number of seats. These schools, however, do not generally operate at full capacity and have much higher operating costs, sometimes two to three times that of mainstream private schools. The pressure to maximize revenue by filling seats is thus really strong. This may mean that some or many of these schools accept children who should not be there, either because their needs are too severe or because they have significant behavioral issues beyond what the school can handle.

Due to the broad spectrum of developmental needs that special needs schools encounter, the benchmarks for success can be murky. In a mainstream school, you can look at where the children get into high school or at test results to get a sense of whether the school is fulfilling its mission. In a special needs school you don't have these markers. You probably won't have a standard curriculum either, so you don't really know what is going on in the classrooms or how to gauge if your child is really learning anything. The curriculum in special needs schools is often very different and very foreign to an outsider. There probably will not be recognizable markers for achievement, nor will you know the extent to which the school actually has and is using the resources, teachers, and therapists it claims to have available to meet the needs of your non-

mainstream child. These schools will often say they can serve a child well, but you should be skeptical. The
right special needs school will look really carefully at your child's strengths and weaknesses and be able to offer clear ideas for appropriate interventions and accommodations. Ask lots of questions. Look very carefully at what happens in the classrooms. Speak with as many teachers and specialists as possible. Each student should have an education plan that is built around their issues. You should ask how these plans are developed and how progress is tracked and measured against plan goals. Ask about their criteria for admission. Be observant. As you walk around you should see classrooms in which the children seem engaged and happy. Ideally there should be no extreme behaviors, but if they do occur, they should be managed quickly and in a humane way. The teachers and administrators should seem accessible, kind and patient, and be able to engage the children. The mission of special needs schools is admirable. What is questionable is the extent to which they can accomplish what they set out to do with the resources they have available.

Progressive developmental schools are an option which falls somewhere in between the mainstream and the non-mainstream. These schools typically have flexible boundaries and expectations. They often classify themselves as schools for creative children, which can be code for children who may be creative but who also have developmental disorders, delays, and behavioral problems. A psychologist once told me that in her experience, many of the children she saw with developmental delays and disorders were creative and non-traditional thinkers, so the idea that these schools serve creative children who also are non-mainstream is not incorrect. For the purpose of schooling, however, the distinction is important. Being creative is one thing, but being creative and developmentally disordered or delayed is something else entirely.

The developmental window for acceptable candidates at progressive developmental schools is usually very broad, so they will have a wide range of abilities in the children they admit. Make sure that if the school is admitting children with developmental disorders and delays, they also appreciate and provide the special accommodations that these children need.

They should have a learning resource center with staff who are able to speak knowledgeably about the special needs served by the school and how they go about serving them. There should be clear boundaries for behavior that are reinforced throughout the school. If non-mainstream children are not well served, like all children, their behavior can deteriorate quickly and disrupt a classroom environment. Having and enforcing a clear and widely understood code of conduct is essential. Some of these schools have grown from parent co-ops and may not have well-established policies and rules. My son attended a progressive developmental school in which a number of the classrooms were profoundly chaotic. He described children walking on desks in his Spanish class and saying wildly inappropriate things to the beleaguered teacher. Fortunately, the school now has a new Head who has put boundaries in place and brought the chaos to an end.

Make sure that the administration is competent. Progressive developmental school administrations can be casual to the point of nonexistence. This may not seem all that important but can be extremely important if there is a problem. If your child is injured and in need of some kind of medical attention, for example, you want to be sure the administrators in the office know what to do and will do it. This may mean just having a box of Band-Aids and antiseptic cream ready in an office drawer, or much more.

Another potential issue is that non-mainstream children can get lost in progressive developmental schools, not really failing but also not really thriving. You must look carefully. Make sure the school understands your child's issues and seems able and willing to accommodate them. Ideally, any school you consider would have experience with issues similar to or the same as those your child faces or at least be able to adapt their resources and expertise to these issues. A progressive developmental school, if well run and appropriate for your child, can be a wonderful open-ended experience and importantly, still sits in the mainstream.

Homeschooling is a very viable option and one with which I have no experience. In our case, I felt that I was already so involved in my son's life that we needed a break from one another and homeschooling would have been too much. School provided a space that for each of us seemed both healthy and necessary. I could have tried to find someone to homeschool my son in our house, or in theirs, or could have joined a group of homeschooling parents who shared the teaching load and essentially created their own tiny school. I regret not having explored these options more fully, as it would have given me huge flexibility and enabled me to efficiently customize my son's education to his specific needs. Everyone I know who has homeschooled a child says that the time spent at classroom learning is so much more efficient that it can be condensed down into a morning, leaving the afternoon free for other activities. If you travel a lot, homeschooling is an interesting option, as it makes your child and their schooling mobile.

A potential concern with homeschooling is that it lacks the institutional protections that should exist in an established school. You do not have an administration to deal with the paperwork, entanglements, and inevitable disagreements and conflicts that occur routinely in a school. You also may not have trained teachers. Your child will be seeing a much smaller number of children, be in a much smaller school community, and have access to fewer resources. If your child is not a good match to or has a problem with a given teacher, for example, there is likely to be no alternative, nor an administration to arbitrate. Homeschooling also requires time. You or someone else will be spending four to six hours per day, four to five days per week with your child, plus additional time for preparation. Coordinating this with a job is close to impossible. If you can, however, find the time, mental space, and energy, then homeschooling might be an interesting option.

Forming your own school is something with which I do have experience. It requires a lot of time and energy and potentially enables you to tailor an entire school curriculum to meet your child's particular needs and interests. This option will require one or several large donors, as the cost of educating non-mainstream children, which is high to begin with, becomes astronomically high at the low enrollment levels you will have in the beginning and for some time thereafter. The range and magnitude of special needs the school serves will have a direct impact on cost. If you are able to define a fairly narrow window of special needs, for example only children with a nonverbal learning disorder, this will lower the resource requirements and subsequently the costs. It will also lower the number of eligible children who can be served, the number of seats that can be filled, and the revenue that follows occupied seats. Serving a wider window of needs will potentially attract more children but is usually more resource intensive and hence more expensive.

If you do not plan to be a major donor, make sure that your child's needs align well with the interests of the major donors. Except in very unusual cases, the donors will ultimately shape the school, what is becomes, and whom it serves.

It takes several years for a new school to establish itself. A school can be put together fairly quickly, but making sure the day-to-day operations and structural backbone run smoothly requires trial and error and will take time. No matter how well educated or well-versed in running schools your founders and initial staff may be, you should be prepared for at least one to two rocky years before your school is running smoothly.

To summarize, when you think about potential school options, the questions you should be asking yourself are:

1. What population does this school serve and is my child developmentally and temperamentally well suited to this group?
2. Does this school really understand its population and serve them well?
3. Can I see my child being happy in this community, in these classrooms, and with these children?
4. Does the school understand the challenges my child faces. Are they willing to work with these challenges in a way that seems credible and committed for the entire duration of my child's tenure at the school?
5. Does the school have the expertise and resources to create a successful and positive learning environment for my child?

What about learning outside of school? Especially now, with ever increasing learning options online, there are a myriad of potentially interesting educational options beyond traditional schooling. Hopefully someday the boundary between being physically "in school" and out will vanish, so that our children's entire world will be an experience from which they, and we, will expect them to be educated.

XII. UNDERSTANDING THE WORLD OF THERAPISTS

Therapists are the foot soldiers of the non-mainstream child's world. They provide the tools and support necessary to perform the tasks of daily life. Some of the areas in which therapists work are speech, auditory processing, and pragmatic social skills such as starting a conversation (speech pathologists or speech therapists); movement, motor skills, flexibility, strength, and balance (physical therapists); fine motor skills such as handwriting, coordination of visual and motor movement, and everyday life tasks (occupational therapists); family dynamics, social interaction, defiant behaviors, emotional and psychological issues (psychologists, counselors, and clinical social workers). Therapists are expensive. Ongoing therapy can become really expensive but there are ways to afford these services, as outlined in Chapter 2. Obamacare and the growing parity of psychological illness with physical illness will hopefully make these services increasingly covered by insurance. In the meantime, you can increase the probability of your insurance company paying at the time of service (or reimbursing you afterwards) if you:

1. Keep a log of your child's therapy appointments: date, provider, what you paid, when you filed the claim, and the amount that is eventually paid by insurance. I recommend that you fax your claims in. This is much faster and reduces the possibility of them getting lost. You will likely have to call your insurance company to get their claims fax number, as it never seems to be on their website or in their literature. Insurance companies are notorious for losing claims and other paperwork, so you should make a copy of anything you send them. After you fax in a claim, if you don't hear back in three

to four weeks call the claims department to inquire what is happening. Keeping a spreadsheet with the details for each claim you file makes this easy. It is also useful to make notes about what is going on and/or any additional documentation needed. Sometimes an insurer will need only a single piece of paper or number to process a claim but it will take them six weeks to tell you.

2. Keep a list of diagnostic and CPT codes that your specialists are using. Every time a specialist makes out a bill there will be a CPT code that indicates what kind of procedure was done, such as a particular exam or test (see footnote 4, page 5). There will also be a diagnostic code that indicates the provider's best assessment of the underlying condition or illness. Some diagnostic codes get higher reimbursements than others, so you will want to keep track of which codes get the highest payouts. Your specialist may know this, or if you are lucky you may be able to get a claims person at your insurance company to tell you. More than likely you will have to learn by trial and error. There is also information on the Internet about which diagnostic codes work best for a given condition and how to manage your insurance claims in general.[11]

3. Appeal any claim that is denied. Every insurer has an appeals process. Usually this means gathering documentation from your specialists and a letter of medical necessity from the overseeing doctor. You will need to call your insurer to ask what to do. It is not hard, just tedious. And often you can win.

Therapists operate in the chasm between your child and the mainstream world, trying to reduce or eliminate the problems that are creating a gap between the two. If your

---

11. See, "Insurance Coverage Tips for Speech and Other Special Needs Therapies." *pursuitofresearch.org*. Pursuit of Research, 2014. Web. 21 July 2014.

experience is like mine, most of your child's therapies will seem vague and meandering. There are the rare exceptions. My son had speech pathologists who set clear goals in monthly work plans and graphed the progress made towards each goal. Cognitive behavioral psychologists are likely to have concrete end points and a clear process as well, as they are targeting specific, identifiable behaviors with very specific interventions. Most therapies, however, are not like this in my experience. Therapy is a process. It has a clear starting point, a fuzzy middle, which is usually not well defined, and an end point, which often is also not well defined, at least not at the start. Once I came to realize this, it began to make a bit more sense. The starting point in therapy is your child today. The end point is better function in the area of weakness. For example, improved handwriting or more enunciated speech, or better coping mechanisms when your child is frustrated are all possible therapy goals or end points. How much improvement can be made and to what extent you can reach the end point is usually not known at the onset. The most effective path to this endpoint is also usually not known from the start, and is often not clear for a large portion of the therapy. I hypothesized that this lack of clarity comes from the fact that the therapist does not usually know where they will have to go with a child to get the improvement they hope to achieve. Nor do they necessarily know to what extent they ultimately can improve a weakness or problem.

The main part of the work in therapy is what happens between the start and end points. This middle will unfold as your child moves forward with the therapy and is not predictable, at least not with much accuracy. Although you cannot always know where the therapy is going or along what path it is preceding, you can and should ask for periodic progress meetings to discuss how your child is doing relative to where they started. You will want to know what has happened or not happened over the last weeks, and where your child is relative to the desired endpoint. An end is usually out there, but you sometimes have to push for it, as there is always something else to work on. I used assessments by teachers, other therapists, and doctors to help me determine whether the benefits of a given therapy continued to outweigh the costs. Therapy can go on for years and its cost is not only monetary. There is the overhead in transportation to and from the therapy, and the opportunity cost of the time your child spends in the therapy and you or someone else spend driving and waiting; time which could be spent doing something else instead. Sometimes there seems to be no end unless you arbitrarily impose one. My son went to speech therapy for seven years until I finally decided to end it. His teacher at school convinced me that his speech was fine and it was crazy to continue. His speech pathologists did not want us to stop but we did. My son's speech was, and is, just fine. More speech therapy could have helped him in some way I am sure, but it was not worth the time, expense, and hassle.

Although the endpoints in therapy may be ambiguous, you should have a clear idea as to why your child is in therapy. You should, for example, understand that your child is seeing a psychologist for anxiety or a physical or occupational therapist because of a difficulty with fine and gross motor tasks. After that, the therapy takes off on its own unique journey somewhere.

How do you know if your child should be in therapy and/or whether the therapist you have chosen is actually helping your child? Therapy is usually recommended by teachers, or the physician or specialist overseeing your child's developmental issues. This could be your primary care doctor, your developmental pediatrician, your psychiatrist, or some other therapist or counselor. They will see something that doesn't seem right and tell you the type of therapist to see and why. Often they can also recommend a particular person.

Knowing if a therapist is helping your child is largely a subjective judgment. You will have hopefully done your homework, by which I mean checking credentials and reviews online and elsewhere. Beyond this, you will have to watch your child over the weeks and months that they are in the therapy. For more simple problems, the benefit of sessions with a good therapist will be visible quite soon, possibly in weeks, depending on the issue. For example, handwriting will improve, or anxiety will be reduced at school, or there will be fewer tantrums at home. The benefits of therapy for harder problems, such as autistic spectrum issues, often don't show up in a child's behavior or thinking for a long time. I would recommend scheduling regular progress meetings every few months or sooner if it seems appropriate. As the paying client, you have a right to know what is going on and this is how you will learn. The therapist should be a good observer of your child. They should be able to describe the various techniques they are using and why and be able to speak in detail about your child's progress towards the end of solving at least part of the problem that brought you there. They should also have a hypothesis as to why the problem is occurring, although they may not know for sure. Finally, they should be willing to share information, answer your questions in a patient and knowledgeable manner, and be willing to tell you if they don't know the answers. As I have said, I am always impressed when a specialist has the self-confidence and humility to say they don't know something, providing they seem to know what they are doing in other areas of course.

Who are these people? They have college degrees and, although it varies somewhat by state, usually also a Master's Degree or post-graduate training (see Appendix D). Most therapists are not physicians and hence cannot prescribe medications. They will not have the depth of medical understanding that you will hopefully see in your child's psychiatrist or pediatrician. They can, however, perform and interpret evaluations and assessments to determine where your child's performance and functioning lies relative to an average cohort of the same age. Therapists also have a remarkable portfolio of tools and gadgets with which to teach and practice skills and work through the various problems and issues that are brought to them. They can be extremely practical and reality based, offering a wealth of solutions to daily problems and challenges.

Psychologists, counselors and clinical social workers are therapists operating in a more esoteric realm. They use a wide variety of approaches, each differing primarily in its assumptions about what motivates human behavior (see Appendix E) and hence how changes and improvements can be made. For example, those using a psychodynamic approach would be interested in understanding the early childhood experiences and unconscious thoughts that created the conflicts assumed to be driving your child's behavior or problem today. Those using a cognitive behavioral approach would want to understand and examine the conscious feelings and thoughts behind your child's problematic behaviors right now, in the present. The humanist approach would focus on understanding the forces acting on your child to impede the innate drive to realize his or her unique self. In this approach the therapist would work with your child to develop an awareness of their unique strengths, which could then be used to correct or redirect a problematic issue or behavior.

Therapists will not usually offer a comprehensive understanding of your child. This is beyond their training and is usually the territory of psychiatrists and behavioral pediatricians. If your child is seeing multiple therapists, you will get multiple and varied perspectives on your child's development which, if you can integrate them into a coherent whole, will begin to tell you something. Over time you will start to gather these fragments into a larger picture of what is happening. Eventually, they will begin to fit together and guide you to where your child is developmentally and what needs to be done to help them. With each therapist, every few months I would ask the questions listed below and then reevaluate my understanding of what was happening.

1. What are you seeing in my child now and do you see a change in their overall level of function?
2. Has your idea of what is going on changed?
3. Has your assessment of whether my child can overcome the problem we are working on changed?
4. What are you focusing on going forward?
5. What else can I be doing to help my child?

XIII. HOW TO FIND, UNDERSTAND, AND USE A PSYCHIATRIST WELL

I have always found psychiatrists intimidating. They are often large, male, and mostly silent, although there are exceptions. Notwithstanding this, we have worked with some remarkable psychiatrists. Over the years their insight and wisdom went far beyond anything I might have hoped for or could possibly have imagined.

Psychiatrists are medical doctors operating in a specialty whose accepted paradigm is under siege (Johnson). Since the late 19th century psychiatry has followed a Medical Model in which human behavior, mood, and thought are attributed to biological causes. For example, hallucinations and fears would be explained by an excess of the neurotransmitter dopamine, or obsessive behaviors would be explained by a deficiency in the neurotransmitter serotonin. Every behavior, emotion, or thought is believed to result from a simultaneous biological process in the brain. Abnormal behaviors are considered to be symptoms of disease resulting from physical (physiological, biochemical, or genetic) causes. In this model, observed symptoms are described, then grouped into clusters and mapped to various illnesses. Once an illness is identified, a diagnosis is made, a prognosis is given, and treatment options follow. In the U.S. the definitive guide for this mapping of psychiatric symptoms onto illnesses is *The Diagnostic and Statistical Manual of Mental Illness* (DSM). The most recent edition of this manual, the DSM-5, has been highly controversial among psychiatrists. Some feel that too many otherwise benign behaviors are now associated with an illness. Others feel that the whole idea of classifying symptoms this way is not useful to begin with, a refutation of the Medical Model itself (Levin). The controversy remains unresolved.

The use of the Medical Model in psychiatry is now being

challenged by a Biopsychosocial Model, in which human behavior is not explained completely by physical causes. In this alternative model, the causes of abnormal behavior and disease also include the web of relationships and circumstances that create the stresses of daily life. Champions of this alternative approach argue that there is no scientific basis to support use of the Medical Model in psychiatry (Gallin). Others argue that the intrinsic validity of psychiatric diagnoses based on subjective descriptions (emotions and thoughts) rather than on physical symptoms is questionable.

Today psychiatrists have two tools for treatment of psychiatric issues: psychotherapy and medication. The use of medication is a natural outgrowth of the Medical Model and its use in the U.S. has been increasing (Brendan L. Smith). Psychotherapy speaks more to the humanistic, social, and holistic interpretations of mental illness. It is still practiced but is becoming harder to get from a psychiatrist. The duration of time a psychiatrist has been in practice is often a reasonable indicator of which of these tools they will favor. Older psychiatrists will have had more training in psychotherapy and less in pharmacology (the science of drugs) and thus are likely to be more comfortable with psychotherapy as the primary treatment approach. Younger psychiatrists will generally have had less psychotherapy training and more training in pharmacology and are thus probably more inclined to favor a medication approach (Taylor). There are the rare exceptions, but psychologists seem to be the main purveyors of psychotherapy today. You can find psychiatrists who use psychotherapy as their principal treatment, but you have to look hard. In my experience, most psychiatrists view medication as the front line approach to treating psychiatric problems.

How do you find a good psychiatrist? If you don't have a referral from a friend, another doctor, or a therapist you trust, I would check the staff rosters of the psychiatry departments in your local hospitals. You are looking for psychiatrists who have specialized or are doing research in areas seemingly relevant to your child's issues. For anyone who seems promising, I would also look at their medical school and residency credentials. Psychiatrists in the U.S. have to complete a four-year residency after medical school and the quality of the program they attend is an indication of their level of mastery in medical school. Psychiatrist resumes are relatively easy to find on the web as well, particularly if the person in question has done research or given lectures and/or talks in their areas of interest, which many of them will have done.

Once you have a name, I would recommend that you speak with the psychiatrist alone and in person before bringing your child in. It is almost impossible to know if a given psychiatrist will be a success until they start working with your child, but you can at least make sure there are no obvious red flags. Some psychiatrists, for example, are more talkative, while others barely speak. Some are more confrontational in their style, asking pointed and direct questions, while others let discussions meander, seemingly without direction or focus. It is important to get a sense of how the psychiatrist thinks about psychotherapy and when and how they use medication. This is difficult to ferret out, as every psychiatrist I have ever asked has said that they use medication only as a last resort. In practice, I have rarely found this to be true.

If your child needs to be on some type of psychiatric medication, such as an antidepressant or antianxiety drug (see Appendix G), a psychiatrist will usually be the doctor to prescribe it. Increasingly, primary care doctors and other types of specialist physicians are writing these prescriptions as well. The wisdom of physicians not trained in psychiatry prescribing psychiatric drugs has been increasingly questioned (Smith 36), but I will leave this topic for another time. If your child needs therapy, you can have a psychiatrist do this if he or she is so inclined and is a good match to your child. An alternative is to have the psychotherapy done by a psychologist or other type of therapist, and limit the psychiatrist's role to managing medication. This is almost always cheaper as psychologist or therapist time is significantly less expensive than psychiatrist time as a general rule. If you choose this route, as many people do, you will have to make sure that both providers speak on a regular basis. It is important that everyone working with your child understands what the others are seeing and doing. It is worth mentioning that insurance companies have historically reimbursed more readily for medication than for psychotherapy, particularly if the psychotherapy goes on for any length of time. You can usually fight this successfully if you would rather your child have more psychotherapy, or a combination of medication and psychotherapy. You will need to request a medical review from your insurance company. Each insurer has a procedure for review that usually requires the potential therapist to fill out a standardized form attesting to the medical necessity of the psychotherapy. I have done this successfully many times. It is not hard.

How do you know if your child needs to see a psychiatrist? If your child is having a problem that is psychological in nature, by which I mean a problem having to do with their thinking, emotions, mood, or behavior, then seeing a psychiatrist is one option for treatment. Seeing a psychologist is another option, although if you think medication might ultimately be needed, this will mean that your child would be seeing both a psychiatrist and a psychologist, which potentially creates problems with coordination of approach. My son started out working with a psychologist. After many years of play therapy with plastic animals, a farmer, and a barn on the floor, he was still having profound problems with attention, so we turned to a psychiatrist for medication. From that point, I looked for psychiatrists who could also do psychotherapy. When we eventually got to a point at which medication was no longer needed, my son went back to seeing only a psychologist.

Some psychological problems emanate from sources external to your child's mind and do not need a psychiatrist, psychologist, or any type of therapist to solve. Children are vulnerable to all sorts of things in their environment. If some external cause is creating your child's issue, then you have been handed a gift, as you may be able to fix the problem without either therapy or medication. A boy in my son's primary school class cried every time the class began a math lesson. A girl in the same class cried when her mother picked her up from school. When the girl got home after school, she ran around the house frenetically. Both of these situations ended up being problems that were fixable without either a specialist or medication. The boy had a learning disability and math was difficult for him.

He was too ashamed to tell anyone and crying helped him release the stress this created. Once he got extra help in math from his teacher and a tutor, his crying stopped. In the second case, the girl was overwhelmed in class. For the first time in her school career she was expected to sit still at a desk and pay attention to a teacher lecturing at the front of the room. The girl was not the only child who found this transition overwhelming, and by the end of the day she cried to release the accumulated tension and frustration from sitting still. The frenetic running around at home was another mechanism for releasing frustration and relieving tension. The fix here was to allow her to get up from her desk, and walk around in the hallway when she felt overwhelmed. This dissipated her stress, made her more comfortable, and stopped the crying and frenzied running around at home. Ultimately, this girl might find that she is ADHD. She could also just be a restless person, which is what the school assumed at that point. It is thus worth trying to identify the source of a problem if you can and whether this source is caused by circumstances external your child's psyche. The psychological symptoms you are seeing may be a result of something in your child's environment, or an illness, or a problem elsewhere in their body, as discussed in an earlier chapter. For example, if your child's school environment is stressful due to a bully operating on the playground or a mean teacher, your child may become withdrawn, depressed, or anxious. Loss of a loved one can cause all sorts of abnormal behaviors and psychological symptoms, such as withdrawal, or crying at small things such as dropping a cookie or finishing a favorite ice cream. Physical illnesses can create psychological problems as well. A gastrointestinal disorder can cause anxiety. An underactive thyroid can cause depression. Excessive irritability and changes in personality can be caused by brain tumors. Without digging a bit for explanations, a child showing symptoms of a psychological nature might otherwise be medicated or counseled into therapy. If you look at your child's life and are able to determine that the problem is not psychological in origin, then you may be able to avoid interventions. Changing schools has been known to eliminate all sorts of anxiety behaviors, depression, and the attention issues that often accompany these conditions. Another example is the experience of my South African nephew. While living in Cape Town he had was put on Ritalin to help improve his attention in school. After his family moved from South Africa to Ireland, a much safer and more peaceful place, he was able to pay attention in his Gaelic school and no longer needed medication. The move eliminated stress created by his worry for his and his family's safety in South Africa. His attention problem was solved by an external change in his environment.

Most psychiatrists treat symptoms. If you can find and treat or eliminate an underlying cause, this is always better than treating symptoms. As mentioned above, attention deficits can be a result of anxiety and will hopefully disappear, or at least become less severe if the underlying anxiety is reduced or eliminated. Treating the anxiety is preferable to treating the attention deficit, which is a secondary effect. The primary cause can often create a cascade of symptoms, making it difficult to identify what is the original problem and what is a result of the original problem. It is easy to get sidetracked into focusing on symptoms instead of primary causes. If you treat symptoms, you are not solving the problem and most importantly you are leaving your child vulnerable to additional symptoms or a worsening of existing symptoms if the underlying cause is triggered again. For my nephew, the underlying condition, anxiety due to fear of living in a dangerous place, was treated when he moved to Ireland. In South Africa, on Ritalin, his symptoms were being treated, but the underlying anxiety resulting from his fear that he and his family might be unsafe remained.

If your child's psychological issues don't seem to be due to external circumstances, some undiagnosed bodily illness, or other non-psychological factor, or if they are but you cannot resolve them, then the next step is to see a psychologist or a psychiatrist. If you believe medication might be helpful at some point or you want a medical perspective that might or might not include psychotherapy, then a psychiatrist is preferable. If you would rather have a broad perspective on how your child thinks, feels, and behaves in the social context of their daily life, then a psychologist is probably a better choice. Most psychologists today view psychological issues through a wide lens, including factors such as the impact of early childhood experiences, cultural influences, learned dysfunctional behaviors, biological factors, internal psychological processes, the drive to realize one's innate potential, and even evolution. It may be possible to find psychiatrists who work through these broad perspectives as well, but it is significantly harder.

If you decide to see a psychiatrist, you will soon discover that psychiatry is a strange animal. In other medical specialties, diagnoses are made based on observable symptoms, which can be tested and measured. The patient is examined, a history is taken, tests are done if appropriate, and a diagnosis is made based on exam, history, and test results. After the diagnosis, a prognosis is given and treatment, usually based on proven methods and practices, is recommended. For example, when your child has a persistent sore throat you can take them to a doctor who will examine them, maybe do a test for strep throat, and then will give you a diagnosis and a prescription if medication is warranted. This methodology of observation, description, diagnosis, and treatment is common across all medical specialties. This is the procedure laid out by the Medical Model. In psychiatry, however, this procedure becomes problematic. Symptoms, for example being depressed or anxious, often may not be directly observable and rarely are measureable. The psychiatrist works from symptom descriptions, which can be biased or distorted, trying to construct a coherent story of what is happening. Diagnoses are made based on the classification and grouping of of symptoms, which are then mapped to a psychiatric illness or condition. A psychiatrist might, for example, see a child whose parents report that for the last six months the child has seemed excessively worried, been restless, irritable, distracted, and easily exhausted most days of the week. This set of symptoms meets the diagnostic criteria for an anxiety disorder and the child could be given this diagnosis. The mapping process is hugely inaccurate, as you might expect, is vulnerable to subjective interpretation, and is controversial, as mentioned (Aboraya).

When you take your child to a good psychiatrist it is likely that they will repeat the exercise I described in an earlier chapter, to determine if your child's issues can be traced to external factors or some other physiological condition. They should ask you and your child questions about your child's daily life and experience, in an attempt to understand if there are environmental factors influencing your child's psychological well-being. Psychiatrists routinely use standard diagnostic tools to measure basic physiological function, such as blood tests to look for chemical imbalances or other medical issues that might explain your child's condition. Less often they may use imaging and brain scans to try to detect disease and brain abnormalities. This phase of your relationship will be relatively concrete. The results of these tests are knowable and will indicate with reasonable accuracy whether there is a physiological issue, such as a thyroid problem, a vitamin deficiency, or an absence seizure. If the psychiatrist determines that your child's issue is due to some physiological condition or external factor, the treatment is usually fairly clear and specific. If the psychiatrist determines instead that the issue is psychological in nature, then the relationship changes. From here the territory becomes murkier, as you are moving from modern, high tech medicine into the realm of educated conjecture. In my experience, from here forward you will typically get vague and inconclusive answers to straightforward questions. I believe this is because the answers in most cases are not known; they are hypotheses. It is totally reasonable to ask the psychiatrist what they think is happening and how things seem to be progressing, but I have rarely gotten a clear answer to these questions.

This vague cloudiness mirrors the inherent ambiguity of psychiatry today. The debate between schools of thought on how psychiatry should be practiced is not yet resolved. Whether a Medical Model or a Biopsychosocial Model is more effective in treating psychiatric issues is still under debate (Lane). In the Medical Model, abnormal behaviors and thoughts are symptoms of psychiatric illnesses caused by changes in the chemistry, structure, and/or organization of the brain. In the Biopsychosocial model, social and psychological factors are considered to be potential causes as well. For a child with depression, following the Medical Model would mean focusing on the biochemical changes in the brain that occur with depression and prescribing an antidepressant or, in very severe treatment resistant cases, electroconvulsive therapy (ECT). Using the Biopsychosocial model, the unconscious emotions of rage, anger, resentment or grief that are believed to be the crux of depression would also be a focus of the child's treatment. The condition might ultimately be treated with medications or ECT but only after broader social factors were considered. Accurate observation and measurement is not possible in either model. As of this date, there is no complete scientific explanation as to how biochemical and neurochemical factors cause abnormal behaviors and mental illness. If psychological and social factors are added, things become even more vague and any sort of accurate measurement is largely impossible. A good psychiatrist will try to piece it all together into a coherent picture. Yet it still may not be correct.

Psychiatrists can only treat symptoms of psychological conditions at this point in time. They prescribe medication and use or recommend therapies that generally have been shown to reduce the particular symptoms of concern in seemingly similar conditions. They do not speak about cures because at this time they do not have cures. Psychiatry does not understand brain function well enough to cure psychiatric issues and illnesses. Fortunately, psychiatry can often reduce the severity of symptoms and dramatically improve patient function. We knew a child who was plagued by fears of turning into other people she knew, or characters she saw in movies or read about in books, which is a form of psychotic thinking. For years this girl was treated with Abilify, an antipsychotic medication. Abilify did not cure her condition but did lessen the symptoms, making them more bearable. Children with ADHD or conduct disorders are increasingly also treated with antipsychotics. Again, the antipsychotics are treating symptoms, damping down the hyperactive behaviors but not curing the underlying condition. Many of the same therapies and medications work for a broad swath of conditions, enabling psychiatrists to take somewhat of a scattershot approach, hoping that something will work but not quite knowing what or why. Once your child sits under a diagnostic category, the range of potential medications and therapies narrows, but diagnoses are often uncertain and can be wrong. Diagnoses also tend to limit a provider's thinking about what is happening, which you will have to be alert to and fight against if you feel a diagnosis or some ramification of a diagnosis is not consistent with what you are seeing. Once a psychiatrist or other specialist has given your child a diagnosis, your child becomes part of this group. This is reasonable, as it gives providers a common language and understanding, focuses their thoughts, and gives them a framework for thinking about and treating what they believe is happening. This also creates the potential danger that the attributes associated with the diagnosis will too easily be attached to your child, sometimes wrongly. For example, a child diagnosed with oppositional defiant disorder would be expected to have frequent tantrums and/or be excessively defiant. Once carrying this diagnosis adults will expect difficult behavior and might not look further at whether the child's behavior is also the result of the hyperactivity that accompanies ADHD, or a learning disorder that causes frustration, or an anxiety disorder that causes the child to be overwhelmed, or something troubling in their environment. You will have to be vigilant, always checking your own hypothesis about what is going on against what providers tell you they believe is happening. If something doesn't fit, then somewhere something is wrong. Your hypothesis may be wrong, the diagnosis may be wrong, or may be correct but with important exceptions. Unlike other branches of modern medicine, psychiatry is still hugely imprecise and rife with uncertainty.

XIV. THE QUESTION OF MEDICATION

The medications I discuss in this chapter are psychotropic medications. This means that they are prescription drugs that alter the brain's chemical function to treat problematic behaviors and other psychiatric symptoms. Some examples include Ritalin and Concerta to treat attention deficit disorder, Lexapro to treat anxiety, and Abilify to treat hyperactivity and psychosis. Other labels for these kinds of medications are psychiatric, psychotherapeutic, or psychoactive.

No sane person wants their child on medication if they can avoid it. Similarly, caring and attentive parents do not want their children to suffer. Herein lies the dilemma. If we knew with certainty that a given psychotropic medication could reduce or eliminate a behavior or symptom that was plaguing our child, it would be easy to make the decision as to whether to medicate. I would not, for example, hesitate to give my son Insulin if he were a diabetic or clotting factor medication if he were a hemophiliac. These drugs have been shown to work for the treatment of these conditions, the correct dosage is known, and the drug's effects can be measured and adjusted when and if necessary. Psychotropic drugs do not share this certainty or accuracy. When they work they can be miraculous, but whether or not they will work is not knowable beforehand. Similarly, the conditions under which one might consider using a given psychotropic drug cannot be measured accurately, nor can the correct dosage of the medication, if it is even to work, be known in advance. Psychiatrists often will not even have complete confidence in their diagnosis and it is not uncommon to have disagreement as to what they are seeing and how it should be treated (Pilgrim).

Most of us have heard about or known children who could not stop whirling around long enough to focus on much of anything. After taking Ritalin, these children were miraculously able to sit quietly and concentrate. There are cases of anxious children cowering behind doors and barely able to function who after taking Lexapro, were able to lead normal lives. The questions arise because the prescribing of psychiatric medications is an educated guessing game based on information that is largely subjective, and on the hard earned experience of your psychiatrist or other prescribing physician.

The uncertainty around these medications is improved somewhat by the grouping of psychiatric medications into classes according to the conditions they have been approved to treat. These classes are:

- Antidepressants
- Anxiolytics (Anti-Anxiety Medications)
- Mood Stabilizers (Anti-Manics, Anticonvulsants)
- Antipsychotics
- Stimulants (ADHD)
- Depressants (Sedatives and Hypnotics)
- Others

This last class refers to a category of medications prescribed in an off-label use. In off-label usage a prescribed drug has been approved for treating one condition, but scientists and doctors then find that it also works for treating one or more other conditions. The drug has not been tested nor approved for these additional off-label uses. Although drug companies cannot advertise the drug for the new uses, it can be prescribed for these other conditions at the discretion of the treating physician. For example, Buspar was approved by the Food and Drug Administration (FDA) to treat anxiety but is also prescribed to treat aggression. Antipsychotics have been approved for treating psychotic disorders and severe childhood behavioral problems but are sometimes also prescribed for ADHD and anxiety. Selective serotonin reuptake inhibitors (SSRI's) are approved to treat depression but are also prescribed to treat migraine headaches and so on.

To me, the question of medication has always been a question of which is worse, my child's symptoms or the possibility of adverse side affects and a negative or even paradoxical reaction from a given drug. It is a calculated gamble. Sometimes things can get bad enough that it is clearly worth the wager, as scary as that may be. When your child is not suffering greatly, the question of whether to try medication becomes much more difficult. You will have the advice of your psychiatrist or other treating physician and possibly other therapists, but in the end only you can make this judgment call. If modern psychiatry better understood the process by which these medications work, you could make this decision with some level of confidence. For now, however, the administering of psychotropic medications is trial and error. You will not know whether a medication is going to work until your child has tried it. When it works it is magical and can completely change your child's experience of the world, for the better. My son described the experience of being on Ritalin for the first time as akin to being a camera that finally was in focus. He went from being a child whose teacher worried that he would never get through the year's math curriculum to being an independent and excellent student. All this because somehow, in that moment, my son's biochemistry and the Ritalin interacted in a manner that caused a dramatic improvement in his attention. This is the positive side of medication. When it doesn't work, it could have no effect, or cause a worsening of the problem being treated, or could introduce a whole new set of symptoms, or your child could have a paradoxical reaction, which is a nightmare.

It is important to recognize, as mentioned earlier, that psychiatric medications do not cure the conditions for which they are prescribed; they only treat symptoms. Because psychiatry does not fully understand the mechanisms by which psychiatric conditions act, the medications it has developed are imperfect. It is often difficult to make reliable psychiatric diagnoses for the same reason. In a manner of speaking, psychiatrists are stumbling around in the dark. What saves them, and us, is the fact that the educated guesswork of a wise and experienced psychiatrist can be remarkably prescient.

So, how do you think about whether your child should be on medication? As said above, no doctor knows whether a given medication will work for your child. They also are not curing your child's problem, only treating their symptoms. They can tell you that a particular medication has worked for other children with seemingly similar symptoms. So, for example, if your child has problems with attention, they can tell you that other children with attention issues have been successfully treated with the stimulants Ritalin, Concerta, Adderall, and Focalin, and that sometimes they have also seen success with antipsychotic medications. To know if a certain medication will work for your child, you will have to try the drug and watch for a result. Sometimes, fortunately not often, the results can be really scary. But as described above, the successes are amazing. It is hard to imagine the added burden that conditions like ADHD, anxiety, and depression can impose on a child. When a medication works the difference can be profound across many dimensions. This is what justifies the risks, sometimes, maybe.

The question of medication is a problem of cost and benefit. The potential benefit of a medication that works is extraordinary, but the cost you will pay is at least the period of uncertainty through which you must pass before you know if the medication does or does not work. If a given medication doesn't work, the cost can be much higher, and if you had known this with hindsight you never would have tried it. You might get lucky and a given drug might work the first time your child tries it. Your child also might have a paradoxical reaction that could make them feel much, much worse and cause them to behave in possibly weird and disturbing ways. You don't know what the outcome will be. Even if the medication is a success, it can still have side effects that make it unacceptable. For example, certain anti-psychotics cause severe weight gain. Certain anti-anxiety medications can cause confusion, impaired judgment or depression. In cases where significant adverse side effects are seen, even if the medication works to reduce the targeted symptoms, it has to be stopped (see Appendix G, Potential Side Effects).

The cost of not trying medication extends beyond avoiding the possible bad side effects. The loss in your child's well-being and function as they continue to be unwell can be profound. All of the time your child is suffering is a tax on their being, function and development. A tax that precludes them from growing and thriving to the extent they otherwise might. If anxious, your child may not play with peers, compromising the development of important strategic, social, and pragmatic skills. If attention is the issue, your child could miss important lessons in school. The trade-off eventually becomes clear. As said above, sometimes a child is so unwell and miserable that even the possibility of being better seems worth the risk and a medication trial becomes an easy decision. If your child is floating along somewhere between not being completely miserable but not functioning really well either, then whether to medicate becomes more of a philosophical question. In these cases, my personal preference was to try medication. I felt the risk was worth it for the potential benefit. You will have to understand where this decision comes down for you.

The benefit of trying medication is the possible improvement in your child's symptoms. As cited above, the anxious child becomes less anxious, or not anxious at all. The ADHD child is able to sit still for an extended period, maybe for the first time in their life. The depressed child is able to see a world that is not dark. These are powerful outcomes. For a concerned parent, missing an opportunity to have such a result is heart wrenching, but putting your child at risk of becoming even more unwell on a trial medication is also heart wrenching. In many ways, the question of medication is an impossible choice.

If you do decide to try medication, there are a few important guidelines you should follow. Keeping a log of your child's behavior and state of wellness each day is essential. You will think that you will remember, as I did, but you won't. Your psychiatrist or other prescribing doctor will rely on your assessment to determine how effective the medication is, so you will need some system for annotating what you see. There are many ways to make effective annotations. Daily notes are one method, although it is difficult to make comparisons from subjective comments. You want to be able to make comparisons and see trends, to assess if things are worsening, improving, or staying the same over time. The system of annotation I arrived at is probably too detailed for most people, but it worked for me. I chose to track something that was a reasonable indicator for the problematic behavior or condition we were trying to change. I then observed the proxy every day at roughly the same time and twice a day. For example, if your child's issue is attention, you might track the number of times they get distracted while doing homework over the course of an hour. Or, you might observe how many minutes it takes them to dress or undress each day. You want to find something that you can easily observe and can count in whole numbers, (e.g. number of minutes to dress, number of times got up, et cetera). What you track should move up or down with whatever condition the medication is trying to improve, (in the above case, with attention). An illustration of how this would look for a trial of a medication to improve attention is shown in Table 1.

Table 1
Documenting a Medication Trial – Improving Attention

Day	Time of Observation	Value of Proxy (e.g. times distracted from homework in 1 hour)	Average of Proxy Values Each Day	Notes & Side Effects
1	8 am	6	7	No change
1	7:15pm	8	-	Seems a bit agitated
2	8:10am	6	6	No change
2	7:30	6	-	Seems calmer

Day	Time of Observation	Value of Proxy (e.g. times distracted from homework in 1 hour)	Average of Proxy Values for Day	Notes & Side Effects
3	8 am	4	3	Calmer
3	7 pm	2	-	No change
4	8:15am	2	2	Seems fine
4	7:05pm	2	-	Seems fine

If your child is trying a medication to improve an oppositional disorder, the proxy might be the number of interruptions during a meal, or length of time they argue during the drive to school. This type of measurement is not extremely accurate, as you are not controlling for other variables, such as what is interesting, or distracting, or irritating at the moment of your observation. It should though be able to capture improvement over time if it happens. After taking data for ten days, I averaged the two proxy observations for each day and graphed this average against the number of days from the start of the medication. The x-axis of my graph was number of days from the start of the medication trial and the y-axis was the value of my proxy, in this case number of times distracted. Table 2 illustrates how this would look. Based on the graph in Table 2, I would conclude the medication was working. My proxy, (number of times distracted

Table 2
Graphing a Medication Trial

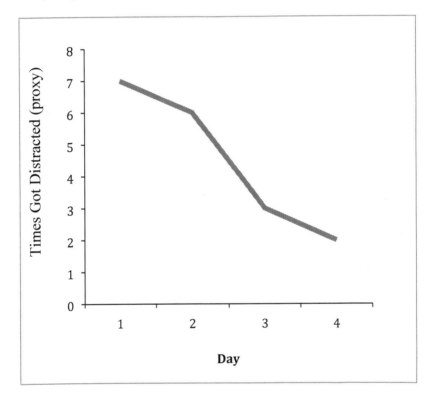

while doing homework) decreased. This meant that my son was sitting for longer periods of time, which meant that he was probably paying attention for longer periods of time. On this medication his attention improved.

You may not want to get this involved, in which case a simple alternative is to write a subjective assessment each day and assign numbers (-3, -2, -1, 0, 1, 2, 3) or words (much worse, worse, same, better, much better) to indicate your child's state of well-being relative to where they were on other days of the trial and before taking the medication. This too can be graphed. The scale you use does not really matter, providing you can consistently indicate a relative worsening or improvement of your child's symptoms. How your child's state of well being was before taking the medication is your baseline and everything is measured against this. You also want to notice if there seem to be any side effects, either good or bad. Your physician should have told you the most common side effects to look for, but there could be others as well.

If you do try medication, when should you decide to end a medication trial? Your doctor will have a point of view on this, as many of these drugs take 2-3 weeks to reach what is called the therapeutic dose and then an additional few weeks to work. Your child will most likely start the trial at a low dose and, providing there are no bad side effects, the prescribing physician will slowly increase the dose to the level at which the drug is supposed to work. This therapeutic dosage level varies by age and weight. Reasonably, psychiatrists like to have children on a medication long enough to get up to the therapeutic dosage level and then stay at this dosage for at least the amount of time the manufacturer says is required for the drug to act. In all, it could be 6-8 weeks or more before you can tell if a given drug is helping. Providing things are going well, this long time frame is not problematic. The issue comes when things are not going well. For example, when your child is not yet at the therapeutic dose but is starting to seem worse, as happened to us. Several days after my son started a trial of an antidepressant, he developed acute fears, paranoia, and became obsessive compulsive. He could not walk a straight line from one side of a room to the other without fear of something or other. I was not able to pick up a phone, as he needed my constant attention and repeated reassurance that things were ok. I can remember looking at him while we were waiting to see his behavioral pediatrician and thinking that his body was so rigid, angular, and tense that it reminded me of one of Picasso's cubist period paintings. I can also remember thinking that this was not right, no matter what our doctor said. The behavioral pediatrician overseeing our trial wanted to keep going, reasoning that the worsening of symptoms we were seeing would disappear once we reached the therapeutic dose. This is reasonable but if things get bad enough you may, as I did, decide to stop anyway whether or not your psychiatrist, behavioral pediatrician, or whoever is overseeing the medication trial agrees The question was again, how does my child's state of well-being or lack of well-being now compare with how he felt before the trial? Is the cost we are paying now outweighed by the potential benefits we can imagine in the future? If a child has to go through a period of being much worse before the medicine can work, is it worth it? Sometimes a drug will take a child through bad patches before it works. You will have to keep assessing how bad the bad patches really are against how bad the original condition was, and against how much improvement you might eventually see. Where the balance comes down is a subjective judgment. The question to ask if things get bad is how much worse is my child now versus not being on this medication at all, or versus being at a lower dosage? You must trade off how much the potential improvement is worth against what your child is experiencing

Table 3
Assessing a Medication Trial

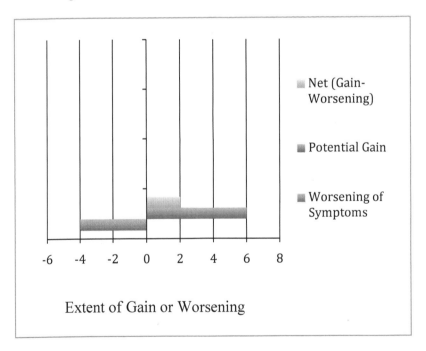

now. If the difference is profound and negative, by which I mean that the potential benefit you can imagine is significantly less than the current worsening of symptoms, then staying on the drug or staying at a given dosage level may not be worth it. Table 3 provides a graphical illustration of this trade-off. As long as you believe the potential gain exceeds the current worsening of symptoms, as shown in Table 3, there is good reason to continue the trial. Again, it is a judgment call that only you can make. Going against the advice of your doctor does not endear you to them but sometimes is necessary. We have done this twice and both times my son was better off without the medication, even though both times the prescribing psychiatrist was against stopping. Once we were set to depart on an overseas trip and my son's symptoms on a particular medication trial had worsened to a point that both our psychologist and our behavioral pediatrician advised us not to travel. My son's behavior was so strange that his psychologist worried that he would not get through airport security. I decided that a change of scenery would be a good thing and we went, against all advice. There was no problem with security and the change of scenery was helpful. I should add that the psychiatrists we liked most were sensitive to worsening conditions on medication trials and usually, although not always, agreed we should end the trial or lower the dose when things got worse. It is important to remember that the psychiatrist or treating physician does not know if being on or off a given medication is better or worse for your child. This will be your determination to make, based on what you see and the advice your providers give you.

Sometimes your psychiatrist may want to prescribe multiple medications. This is problematic as, if something goes wrong, it is hard to tell whether it is due to medication one, medication two, the interaction of the two, or something else. Barring some special circumstance, a single medication should be tried for long enough to see that it works before a second medication is added. You then will have an established baseline against which to measure the effects of any additional medication your child tries.

XV. IF THINGS GET REALLY DARK

Sometimes no matter how hard you try, things get dark. This is less of a problem when children are young, but when they become adolescents it is a big problem. Sometimes parents get to a point at which they understand that their child desperately needs help, but they also understand that they are not able to help them. There are many circumstances that can cause this, but all usually break down to the sad fact that your relationship with your child has degraded to a point at which there no longer is effective communication. As a result, your home and possibly your child's school and community become unhealthy for them. If this happens, your child's ensuing frustration and anger can create circumstances that are dangerously unstable. You want to act sooner rather than later. This situation may take the following forms. Your daughter, who has ADD and has always struggled both academically and socially, has lately become increasingly frustrated and angry. At home, she locks herself in her room. When she does come out, she is hostile and defensive. She lashes out at you and her siblings. She will not talk to you and seems completely locked in her angry darkness. Another scenario is the boy who becomes part of a group that is engaged in risky or self-destructive behaviors. For example, drugs, drinking, skipping school, stealing, and vandalism. Such groups are often made up of adolescents who have been ostracized or in some other way emotionally injured and alienated from their peers and/or the adults around them. When adults try to talk to the boy he will not listen. Eventually, the boy's family becomes worried about his safety in the group.

The circumstances I have heard about are remarkably similar to these examples. An adolescent is mistreated or somehow wounded emotionally, or they let their judgment become distorted by a frustrated and angry peer group making increasingly dangerous choices. Typically, the behavior that ensues is angry and/or destructive. Eventually everything escalates, and the adolescent becomes a threat to their own safety and possibly to the safety of everyone and everything around them. There are things that you can do, but it will take a large shift in perspective to do them. If you have tried all other avenues, are at your wits end, and it still feels that your child needs to be saved, then they probably need to leave home for a while. Ideally, you would like to send them to a place where they can calm down, understand how things went wrong, and become healthy again.

There are a number of excellent wilderness programs for adolescents that will get your child away from home and provide a safe environment in which they can heal and learn. These programs vary in length, depending upon your child's age, temperament, the complexity of their issues, and their willingness to participate. Typical stays range from seven to fifteen weeks. Being outdoors is an important part of these programs, as is intensive exercise each day, such as hiking and rock climbing. Both are felt to cleanse and heal unhappy, disturbed souls. Adolescents go to wilderness programs because they are unreachable, are in some kind of trouble or headed that way, and/or are in pain. As a result, they usually are frustrated and angry. I would strongly recommend that any program you consider be clinically driven. This means that psychologists have designed, manage, and participate in the program and its activities. These programs typically include group therapy and individual therapy. This is helpful, essential actually, because what you have is at least a psychiatric problem that has gotten out of control.

Wilderness programs, like therapy and specialists, are expensive but there are a number of ways to make them affordable. Medical insurance, either private or through Obamacare, is now required to provide mental health benefits commensurate with those for physical illnesses. A wilderness program that is clinically driven is a mental health service and should be covered. Nonprofit organizations such as *SavingTeens* and *Strugglingteens* have scholarships available for adolescents, some paying up to seventy-five percent of wilderness program tuition. Some of the wilderness programs themselves offer scholarships. Medicaid is also a potential source of funds. If you can show your child is not getting the services they need at your local public school, and that a wilderness program is an "appropriate education," your local school district is obligated by law to pay for the program.

If your child goes to one of these programs, you will have to be prepared to be out of contact with them for the first weeks. The number of weeks varies with the program but is typically about three to four. During this time you will be speaking with your child's therapist or counselor on a weekly basis about how your child is doing but you will not be in direct communication with your child. In most programs, you are able to write letters but in the first weeks your child cannot write back. One adolescent we knew was in a program that required him to write a letter of accountability to his parents before he was allowed to write or receive anything else. The hope was that this would open a conversation with his parents about why he was there. His parents could write back, but the letters were vetted by the overseeing psychologist and the parents were strongly encouraged to focus on the most important issues dividing them from their son. Eventually, phone calls between the boy and his parents were allowed, with a therapist also on the line to intervene if the conversation started to get angry, dysfunctional, or began to lapse into platitudes.

The philosophy of these programs is to separate your child from everything that is familiar to them: you, their friends, their home environment, and their things. They are then put in an environment that requires them to take care of themselves on the most basic level to survive. They will be operating with only themselves, their group, their counselors, and their therapists in the wilderness. They will live outdoors, including through the winter, which requires them to focus on their most primitive needs. They are supplied with food, clothing, a sleeping bag, a tarp to sleep on, and whatever other equipment they need for survival. In one program all meals are cooked over a campfire, which was lit by rubbing two sticks together as the Native

Americans used to do. Days are spent hiking, pitching and breaking down camp, meeting with therapists, and working together in various therapeutic groups and activities. The therapy groups are designed to break down whatever anger or dysfunctional behaviors brought these adolescents to wilderness, to make them see the wounds which typically underlie their anger or dysfunctional behavior, and to help them develop healthy tools for coping and moving forward in the world.

Finding these programs and vetting them well is the job of educational consultants. They should know, either by first hand experience or information from colleagues with first hand experience, what really goes on in each program and, importantly, the emphasis of each program. Among others there are programs that focus on physical activity, more spiritual programs that are built around rituals, and programs for adolescents with addictions. Most programs have extensive websites, so you can read about them online. Typically, they are located in Utah and Montana, although there are also a few programs scattered across Maine, New York, and even Hawaii. The venues are very different and each has pros and cons. The Utah programs are typically in the mountains, with lots of hiking and outdoor camping. Other programs emphasize extreme athletics, or community living, or adventure and challenge. You want to be sure that you have picked a reputable program that is as compatible with your child as possible. Once your child leaves home, they are completely in the hands of the program staff, so you need to choose carefully, really, really carefully. Whether or not you use an educational consultant, and you don't necessarily need one, double-check any programs you are considering thoroughly. This means speaking with parents whose children have attended the program, (the programs should be able to give you references), checking online reviews, and speaking with the psychologist or therapist who would be overseeing your child during their stay.

Good wilderness programs are near miraculous in their ability to rid adolescents of their anger, help them understand the underlying wounds behind their anger, and provide the tools with which to cope in the future. They are grueling and difficult but can be rewarding and life-saving. The right wilderness program can make a monumental difference. It can save your child.

XVI. RESIDENTIAL TREATMENT CENTERS AND THERAPEUTIC BOARDING SCHOOLS

An important fact about residential treatment centers (RTCs) and therapeutic boarding schools is that none, or almost none, of the students who are there want to be there. Children and adolescents are sent to these institutions because they have just completed a wilderness program but still need reinforcement of the skills they learned, or because they are not functioning in a healthy or safe manner at home, or because their parents can no longer handle or don't want any longer to handle them at home, or in some cases as an alternative to juvenile hall. Both RTCs and therapeutic boarding schools are residential programs that combine therapy and school in a single setting. Residential treatment centers, as the name suggests, are mostly about treatment, although there also is a school program. They tend to be small and intimate, sometimes with no more then eight to twelve students living in a house, plus counselors, therapists, and teachers. Therapeutic boarding schools put more emphasis on school and are more like traditional boarding schools in size, routine, and physical layout. They offer group and individual therapy in addition to a school program. Children and adolescents in RTC and therapeutic boarding school programs typically are there for drug or alcohol abuse, or for severe behavioral or psychological issues that are beyond the scope of what can be handled at home or in a regular school program. They may have been headed on a path that seemed dark and moving towards a bad place, or have had a community of friends that seemed unhealthy, or might have been struggling with a psychological issue such as anxiety, autism, or bipolar disorder. Younger children typically enter RTCs and therapeutic boarding school programs because they have psychiatric illnesses, or emotional, sexual, or behavioral issues which cannot be treated comfortably at home or which require more intensive treatments and interventions. Children who are sent to these programs typically have complicated psychological issues that have isolated them from their peers and made it difficult for them to focus and participate in school. Eventually their frustration and loneliness builds up to a point that makes them angry, dark, and usually unreachable. Their parents, fearing that they are headed down a path that will end up in a very bad place, want them in a more intensive treatment setting that they hope will help them.

Whether these institutions actually help the children they purport to serve is questionable. They do act as holding places for children who have become unbearable, profoundly disturbed, or in some other way difficult to have at home. In principle, a school that offers therapy should be helpful. What actually appears to happen, however, is something quite different. These institutions operate on a strict behavioral model. Upon entering, a child is severely restricted, to the point of having almost no privileges. They then have to earn these privileges back by demonstrating good and healthy behavior. At one RTC, the children initially are not allowed to leave a room without an escort, nor can they be alone at any time during the day, except when using the bathroom or sleeping. At night school staff sit outside each child's bedroom. Good behavior is rewarded, or conditioned, by increasing privileges. As behavior improves, which is demonstrated by meeting the goals preset by the school, autonomy increases. There is no deviation from the preset goals, nor can they be questioned. The institutions have defined what is healthy, appropriate behavior, and if it is not followed the children remain severely restricted. As a behavior modification technique, this regime is very effective. It is, however, a less effective technique for getting beyond the relatively straightforward forcing of certain behaviors to an understanding of the more complex question of why the dysfunctional behaviors happened in the first place. There is a therapy component to these programs that claims to address this question, but given the strict behavioral regime, I would question whether any child can feel comfortable speaking honestly about their thoughts and feelings. If they say something that a therapist or counselor considers unhealthy, they risk not meeting a new goal or worse, being penalized and losing privileges they have already earned

The paradox of these institutions is that they operate with a strict code of conduct that requires absolute compliance while still calling themselves therapeutic. Getting better is demonstrated by increasing compliance with this code. While being helpful in some ways, a strict behavioral code is not necessarily helpful in solving the kinds of problems for which children have been sent to these institutions, in fact it may work to the contrary. Children and adolescents who enter are typically unhappy, or disturbed, or both. They may not, or potentially will not, or cannot comfortably follow the code of conduct required to meet the school's goals. This results in penalties, typically the downgrading of privileges, which then can cause depression, withdrawal, and defiant behavior. This demonstrates that the child is still not well, needs to continue in the institution, and the cycle starts all over again. These institutions are thus self-reinforcing. Good behavior and compliance with rules and goals is synonymous with good health in this world. As children satisfy goals, they move up a hierarchy, with the goals becoming more nuanced and sophisticated and the privileges continuing to increase. If a student regresses in behavior or attitude, they are downgraded to a more restrictive level and lose the privileges they have earned. They then have to start over to earn the privileges back, which will demonstrate they are getting better and becoming more healthy.

The goals are a mixture of behavioral, developmental, and educational milestones carefully crafted to guide students slowly back to a healthier, more compliant, controlled, and socially appropriate level of function. The net effect of this system is to create a tight web around each student. Until they act in accordance with the rules, they are kept tightly restricted. A failure to follow rules and meet goals is punished with a tightening of the web. Certainly growth of the humanist's individual and unique self is impossible here. Whether any really constructive therapeutic relationship can develop in these institutions is also questionable. These are, however, not environments designed to nurture the unique self or resolve complex therapeutic issues. These institutions are designed to bring extreme behaviors back to a socially acceptable level.

Once this happens, it is reasoned that a child or adolescent can then begin to move forward as a more healthy individual and can live and function appropriately outside the institution.

Building an experience around adherence to a strict code of conduct in a highly restricted environment is a questionable path to improved well-being. Using a code of conduct as a proxy for good health is also questionable. For a creative child, or any child who thinks independently, these institutions are tortuous. For a psychologically disturbed child, the requirements of these institutions can be impossible and crushing.

There is also the question of medication. Each of these schools has a medical director whose job it is to oversee the health of the school community. RTCs tend to be small and can generally handle all sorts of behaviors without resorting to medication as a control mechanism. Therapeutic boarding schools, however, are significantly larger and have the problem of managing the behavior of larger numbers of children, all of who have some sort of behavioral or psychological issue. In these environments, it is easy to understand how medication would become an easy tool for maintaining appropriate behavior. Children who might otherwise not be medicated might, for example, be given antipsychotics or other mood stabilizing medications to dampen behaviors that could otherwise become inappropriate and disruptive to the school community. The threshold for when medication is used thus becomes much lower in these institutions, as the criteria are not just improving symptoms of the individual child but also keeping the community as a whole in as serene and healthy a state as possible.

I question whether these institutions actually help the children they serve. They do provide a place for children and adolescents whose behavior has become too extreme for normal daily life at home or at a non- therapeutic school. This, however, is not the mission they claim.

XVII. STAYING SANE

If you have gotten to this section you either have been through the experiences described in earlier chapters, or have hopefully at least read about them here. This is now the point at which to take stock of yourself, your child, your family, and your life. You have a child who is different and as a result both of you have a life that is either somewhat or very different from that of your peers and your child's peers. You have most likely had to make accommodations, are probably significantly more stressed, and your life probably is significantly heavier than other parents you know. Your child's complications may be modest or significant, but either way your parenting will hopefully have adapted to meet their needs. What you need to do now is to remember a few really important things. Children are children no matter what their issues and capabilities. They need attentive and accepting parents who will give them praise, approval, respect, and unconditional love. The way in which you respond to your child will directly affect their sense of themselves, their self worth, and their behavior. You will need to find a way to see past your child's issues to the person who is there inside. This is often one of the most difficult challenges of having a non-mainstream child. Sometimes your child will seem or look really weird, and will do things that you could not possibly have imagined nor understand.

You must also make a choice as to whether to keep one foot in the mainstream and shuttle back and forth to your child or cast the mainstream aside and move with your child along a different and untested path. How well you come to terms with the fundamentally disparate facts that you have a child operating in one world and you are standing in another will determine the extent to which you can stay sane. In my experience, the mainstream world was often a hostile place for non-mainstream children. I tried to create our own separate and safe world but that was really only possible while my son was young. Once he entered school our separate and safe place was largely gone and I was thrown into shuttling back and forth between worlds. I could have chosen to move off the mainstream at that point, but I chose instead to try to stay on it. My choice had mixed consequences, many good and some very bad.

Understanding what you believe about parenting on a very basic level can help guide your choice of whether you want to shuttle between worlds or cast aside the mainstream world around you and your child. If you are someone for whom rules and decorum are important, then you will likely be more comfortable trying to stay in the mainstream. If you are someone for whom free flowing discovery is important and uncertainty is not daunting, then you should consider stepping off the mainstream. Either way you will eventually have to grapple with the reality that for the next fifteen to twenty years, you and your child will be struggling to build a relationship with the mainstream that works for both of you, and hopefully for your family as well. To me, despite trying to stay in the mainstream, it felt as if we were operating in a parallel universe for much of my son's childhood. Eventually, circumstances forced reality to come crashing down upon us. This was terrifying for me. But my son, after many struggles, picked himself up and moved forward, completely on his own. It is interesting to me that now, operating successfully in the mainstream, he remains non-mainstream at heart and this is one of his greatest creative strengths. A strength born from weakness.

You will likely have friends, as I do, whose children are heading off to Exeter and Harvard. Although I am happy for them, this can be and often is extremely depressing. The idea of an education of that quality and a community of that level of ability is magical. But I came to see that this would not be our path. When I meet the way too self-satisfied mother of one of my son's preschool classmates in the local market, I do not have the ammunition provided by being able to say my child is in a prestigious boarding school or college. I do not have the warm reassurance that my child is moving forward, accumulating the markers of mainstream success. What I do have is the knowledge that my child is unique and gifted in ways that don't fit comfortably into the system of educational and social hurdles our children must move through. And there is always the small satisfaction that for a not insignificant number of its graduates, Harvard is the last accomplishment of note, while for many non-mainstream children, leaving school is just the beginning of really interesting work and a really unique and satisfying life.

What about you? Through all of this, keeping a part of yourself for yourself is essential and may also be close to impossible. I was not able to do this successfully until much later. I am hoping, however, that reading this you will do better than I. With hindsight, I think that sometimes you just have to drop everything and pay attention to yourself. I am not sure how else it can be done. For years there was rarely a moment in which some aspect of my son's world was not at the forefront of my thoughts. As a result, I was distracted and preoccupied for much of that time, missing a lot of the world and the people I cared about around me.

You likely have a partner. If so, this is yet another variable in the mix and another set of demands on you that have the potential to make you crazy. If you are able to create a real collaboration, in which the raising of your child is truly a joint activity, then you have a chance at making your relationship an asset instead of yet another tax. You have the possibility of avoiding the resentment that floats like a specter waiting to descend upon each of you. By joint, I mean your parenting is an activity that consumes both of you, maybe not the same way in kind but definitely the same or near the same way in measure. You may not both be making the seemingly endless drives to therapy appointments, but if one drives to therapy the other should do something close in time and importance. Time is the precious commodity to be bartered. It is time that is taken away from you with a child, and even more so with a non-mainstream child. What I am proposing is not easy, but the alternatives are far worse.

Finally, a critical ingredient in staying sane is keeping a clear, unfettered perspective. If your experience is like mine, you will be told all sorts of bad news. One specialist will tell you that your child cannot do this, another will say they can't do something else. This is wrong, that is not working, some other thing is a problem, and to properly address all of this you will need to be shuttling your child to expensive and time consuming therapies of one sort or another multiple days of the week into the indefinite future. When this happens, as it likely will at some point, you must remember that your child's specialists in most cases don't really know why what they are seeing is happening. This means that they can't really know what the prognosis will be and they can't really know how bad today's deficits will look tomorrow. I have the strong impression that specialists tend to err on the side of being more negative than positive, as I too might if I had no clear idea of what was really going on. Although this is crazy making when you are trying to understand how to help your child, it is a gift when you are hearing about all sorts of problems and endlessly dismal predictions. Nearly every time a specialist told me that my son would not be able to do something, he was not only eventually able to do it but he also usually excelled. This is the paradox of non-mainstream children. It is both crazy making and fascinating.

XVIII. WHAT THE FUTURE MAY HOLD

No one knows what the future holds for any child and non-mainstream children are no exception. What is different in the non-mainstream world is that the possibilities are way more extreme. You may have the next Bill Gates, or you might have a child who will never be able to entirely escape their disorder and the deficits it creates. Or, most likely, you will have a child who falls somewhere in between. You just don't know

You are living with a huge amount of uncertainty, but you must remember that it is uncertain. It is not determined. You have a lot of room to influence what happens. With careful thought and study, the help of talented specialists, the careful following of wise therapy recommendations, and a lot of positive and loving encouragement on your part, the future may be really bright. You will though have to hold a range of possibilities in mind. You will need to live with a level of uncertainty that has probably been unknown to you before now. Even with the best specialists you can find, the answers will not be clear for a very long time, if ever. Somehow you have to manage the extremes of emotion this evokes. It is an unrelenting roller coaster ride for a long, long time. A lot of adrenalin flows. But every hurdle surmounted is a triumph. And there is no reason why you should not have many.

A few essential things to remember. No one knows your child better then you. No matter how prestigious the doctor or therapist, if what they say does not make sense get a second opinion. If the second opinion does not seem right, step back and re-analyze what you know and what you think is happening. Maybe you need to see a doctor or therapist in a different specialty. Maybe the doctors you are seeing are focusing on the wrong information. Remember that they are working from your and their own observations, which can be fallible.

Finally, it is imperative that you feel comfortable with

what you are doing for your child. Only you can see the full picture well enough to make the decision as to what is most likely to help them. Only you know your child across the full spectrum of activities, feelings, and behaviors that make up their world. You may not be right, but if you leave it to your doctors, they might not be right either. And given the choice, I would bet on you first.

APPENDICES

APPENDIX A: DEVELOPMENTAL MILESTONES

A rough guide to the milestones that pediatricians use to assess whether a child is developmentally where they should be by age is listed in Table 4.

Table 4
Developmental Milestones by Age

Age	Social & Emotional	Language	Thinking& Learning	Movement & Physical
2 Mths	• Smiles at people • Can calm self • Looks at parents and care givers	• Coos, gurgles • Turns head to sounds	• Watches faces • Follows things with eyes • Recognizes people • Acts bored when activity does not change	

Age	Social & Emotional	Language	Thinking & Learning	Movement & Physical
4 Mths	• Smiles un-prompted • Likes to play with people • Copies facial expression and movement • Indicates if happy or sad • Responds to affection	• Begins to babble • Copies sounds • Cries in different ways to show hunger, pain, and fatigue	• Reaches for toy with one hand • Uses hands and eyes together • Follows moving things with eyes • Watches faces closely • Recognizes familiar people and things	• Holds head up • May roll over • Pushes down on legs when feet are on a hard surface • Can hold toy and shake it • Puts hand to mouth and elbows • Pushes up on elbows when on stomach

Age	Social & Emotional	Language	Thinking & Learning	Movement & Physical
6 Mths	• Knows faces • Plays with others • Responds to others' emotions • Looks at self in mirror	• Copies sounds • Strings vowels together • Can respond to own name • Makes sounds showing joy and sadness	• Looks at things • Brings things to mouth • Shows curiosity • Tries to get things that are out of reach • Passes things from one hand to the other	• Rolls over • Begins to sit up without help • Can support weight on legs when standing • Rocks and crawls

Age	Social & Emotional	Language	Thinking & Learning	Movement & Physical
9 Mths	• May fear strangers • May be clingy with familiar adults • Has favorite toy	• Under-stands "no" • Makes a lot of sounds • Points at things • Copies sounds and gestures	• Plays peek-a-boo • Moves things smoothly from one hand to the other • Uses thumb and index finger to pick things up • Watches as things fall • Looks for things has seen you hide	• Stands holding on • Can sit by self • Pulls self to standing • Crawls

Age	Social & Emotional	Language	Thinking & Learning	Movement & Physical
1 Yr	• Shy with strangers • Cries when parent leaves • Has favorite things and people • Can be fearful • Hands you a book when wants a story • Repeats sounds, actions for attention • Helps with dressing	• Can respond to simple spoken requests • Shakes head for no • Waves good-bye • Says "mama," "dada" • Tries to say words you say	• Explores by shaking and banging • Finds hidden things easily • Identifies pictures • Copies gestures • Starts to drink from cup • Puts things in and takes things out of containers • Pokes with index finger • Follows simple directions	• Gets to sitting position without help • Pulls self up to standing • Walks holding on to things • May stand alone or take a few steps alone • Bangs things

Age	Social & Emotional	Language	Thinking & Learning	Movement & Physical
18 Mths	• Likes to hand things to others	• Says several single words	• Points to body parts	• Walks alone
	• May have tantrums	• Says and shakes head "no"	• Scribbles alone	• May walk up steps or run
	• Shows affection to familiar people	• Knows common objects by name	• Can follow 1-step verbal commands	• Helps to undress self
	• Points to show things of interest or to get attention		• Pretends to feed dolls or animals	• Pulls toys while walking
	• Explores alone with adult nearby		• Points to show something wanted	• Drinks from a cup
				• Eats with a spoon

Age	Social & Emotional	Language	Thinking & Learning	Movement & Physical
2 Yrs	• Copies others • Gets excited when with other children • Acts with more autonomy • Shows defiant behavior • Plays next to other kids	• Knows names of people and body parts • Says 2-3 word sentence • Follows simple directions • Repeats words • Names items in book • Finishes sentences and rhymes	• Builds block towers • Follows 2-step directions • Finds hidden things • Begins to sort shapes and colors • Plays simple games • Points to things in books • Copies straight lines, circles	• Stands on tiptoe • Kicks a ball • Begins to run • Climbs onto things alone • Walks up and down stairs holding on • Throws ball

Age	Social & Emotional	Language	Thinking & Learning	Movement & Physical
3 Yrs	• Copies adults and friends • Shows affection • Takes turns • Shows empathy for crying friend • Knows "mine," "yours," "his," "hers" • Separates easily from parents • May not like changes in routine • Dresses, undresses self	• Can name most things • Under-stands "in," "on," "under" • Says age, first name, sex • Names a friend • Says "I," "me," "we," "you" • Talks clearly • Can have 2 to 3 sentence back and forth • Follows 2-3 step directions	• Plays pretend with dolls, people, animals • Does 3 to 4 piece puzzles • Can understand the word "two" • Turns pages of book • Builds towers of more than six blocks • Turns door handles • Screws and unscrews jars	• Climbs well • Runs easily • Pedals a tricycle • Walks up and down stairs • Can use buttons, levers, moving parts

Age	Social & Emotional	Language	Thinking & Learning	Movement & Physical
4 Yrs	• Enjoys doing new things • Plays mom and dad • Is more creative in play • Prefers to play with other children • Cooperates with others • Knows real from make-believe • Tells likes and interests	• Knows basic grammar • Sings and recites poems from memory • Tells stories • Can say first, last name • Names colors, some numbers	• Can count • Starts to understand time • Can remember part of a story • Knows same and different • Draws people with 2 body parts • Starts to copy capital letters • Plays board, card games	• Hops • Stands on one foot up to 2 seconds • Catches a bounced ball • Pours • Cuts and mashes own food • Uses scissors

Age	Social & Emotional	Language	Thinking & Learning	Movement & Physical
5 Yrs	• Wants to please • Wants to be like friends • Likely to agree with rules • Likes to sing, act and dance • Shows concern and sympathy • Knows male and female • Is sometimes demanding and sometimes cooperative	• Speaks clearly • Tells simple story with full sentences • Uses future tense • Says names, address	• Counts 10 or more things • Can draw person with six body parts • Can print some letters, numbers • Copies triangles and other shapes • Knows about money, food, and other everyday life things	• Stands on one foot for 10 sec • May skip • Can somersault • Can use toilet alone • Swings and climbs

Source: "Developmental Milestones." *CDC 24/7: Saving Lives, Protecting People.* Center for Disease Control and Prevention, 27 March 2014. Web. 7 July 2014.

APPENDIX B: DEVELOPMENTAL TESTING

Developmental testing, or screening, is a set of standardized tests designed to detect developmental delays and disorders. Table 5 details the principal tests endorsed by the American Academy of Pediatrics. Your pediatrician will decide on which tests to administer based on the issues of concern, your child's age and race, and the cost, time, and difficulty of administering the test.

Table 5
Developmental Testing by Age

Test	Areas Evaluated	Age	Other Considerations
Ages & Stages Questionnaire	• Communication • Gross and fine motor skills • Problem solving • Personal adaptive skills	4 - 5 Yrs	• Parent questionnaire • Graded pass/fail
Battelle Developmental Inventory Screening Tool (BDI-ST)	• Communication • Cognitive Development • Motor skills • Personal, social adaptive skills	0 - 8 Yrs	
Bayley Infant Neuro-developmental Screen (BINS)	• Articulation • Language • Gross and fine motor skills • General knowledge, • Personal and social skills	3 - 24 Mths	• Graded low risk/ moderate risk/ high risk in each category

Test	Areas Evaluated	Age	Other Considerations
Brigance Screens-II	• Articulation • Language • Gross and fine motor skills • General knowledge • Personal and social skills, • Pre-academic skills	0 – 6 or 0 -7 Yrs	• All results are criteria-based • No normative comparisons
Capute Scales, also called Cognitive Adaptive Test or Clinical Linguistic Auditory Milestone Scale (CAT/CLAMS)	• Problem solving • Language • Visual-motor skills	3 Mths - 3 Yrs	
Checklist for Autism in Toddlers (CHAT)	• Detects children at risk for autism	18 Mths - 2 Yrs	• Parent questionnaire • Graded pass/fail
Child Development Inventory (CDI)	• Social skills • Self-help skills • Language • General development	18 Mths - 6 yrs	• Parent questionnaire

Test	Areas Evaluated	Age	Other Considerations
Child Development Review-Parent Questionnaire (CDR-PQ)	• Social skills • Self-help skills • Motor skills • Language skills	18 Mths - 5 Yrs	• Parent questionnaire • Graded no problem/ possible problem/ major problem
Denver-II Developmental Screening Test	• Language • Gross and fine motor skills	0 - 6 Yrs	• Pass/fail for each question • Normed for age • Graded normal/ suspect/ delayed
Early Language Milestone Scale (ELM Scale-2)	• Speech and language development	0 - 3 yrs	
Early Motor Pattern Profile (EMPP)	• Movement • Tone • Reflex development	6 Mths - 1 Yr	• Yields normal/ suspect/ abnormal
Infant Development Inventory	• Social and self-help skills, • Language • Motor skills	0 - 18 Mths	• Parent questionnaire • Graded delayed/ not delayed

Test	Areas Evaluated	Age	Other Considerations
Modified Checklist for Autism in Toddlers (M-CHAT)	• Detects children at risk for autism	26 Mths - 4 Yrs	• Parent questionnaire • Graded pass/fail
Motor Quotient (MQ)	• Gross motor development	8 – 18 Mths	
Parent Evaluation of Developmental Status (PEDS)	• Screen for developmental and behavioral problems	0 - 8 Yrs	• Parent questionnaire • Graded referral/ additional screening/ continued monitoring
Pervasive Developmental Disorders Screening Test II (PDDST-II) Stage I- Primary Care Screener	• Screen for detection of children at risk for autism	1 – 4 Yrs	• Parent questionnaire • Graded pass/fail
Pervasive Developmental Disorder Screening Test II (PDDST-II) Stage 2 - Developmental Clinic Screener	• Screen for detection of children at risk for autism and other developmental disorders	1 - 4 Yrs	• Parent questionnaire • Graded pass/fail

Test	Areas Evaluated	Age	Other Considerations
Screening Tool for Autism in Two-Year Olds (STAT)	• Second-level screen for detection of autism and other develop-mental disorders • Behaviors in play, requesting, directions • Attention • Motor domains	2 – 3 Yrs	
Social Communication or Autism Screening Questionnaire (SCQ or ASQ)	• Identifies children at risk for autistic spectrum disorders	0 - 4 Yrs	• Parent questionnaire • Graded pass/fail

Source: "Identifying Infants and Children with Developmental Disorders in the Medical Home: An Algorithm for Developmental Surveillance and Screening." *Pediatrics* 118 (2006): 405-420. Web. 10 August 2014.

APPENDIX C: POTENTIAL SOURCES OF FINANCIAL ASSISTANCE

I have tried to answer the question of how to afford all of this in Chapter 2. A summary of those ideas is listed in Table 6.

Table 6
How to Afford Services and Specialists

Option	Notes
Medical Insurance	• Obamacare covers some testing • Obamacare should cover "medically necessary" services, specialists, and therapies
Specialist Sliding Scale	• Some specialists may reduce fees for lower income families • Often must ask
Medicaid	• May pay for some services but must qualify
State Children's Health Insurance Plan (SCHIP)	• For families whose income is too high for Medicaid but is still below state cut-off limits
Private Funding Organizations	• Offer aid, behavioral health loans, and scholarships for wilderness programs and therapeutic boarding schools • See *SavingTeens.com,* • See *Strugglingteens.com*

Table 6 How to Afford Services and Specialists	
Option	Notes
Public Schools	• Must offer "free appropriate education in least restrictive environment possible" • Must provide services and/or pay for other schools and programs, (for school age children), if cannot provide what child needs
Community Health Centers	• See SAMHSA Behavioral Health Treatment Services locator online, *findtreatment.samhsa.gov*, for the center closest to you • Likely to offer more affordable services and specialists
National Alliance on Mental Health (NAMI), Mental Health America (MHA)	• Advocacy groups offering help locating services
Universities and Colleges	• Those offering psychiatry, psychology, social work, counseling, and/or therapy programs may have clinics offering services for a reduced rate or for free
Group Therapy	• Is less expensive than individual therapy

Source: Katie Kerns. "6 Cheap Ways to Get Mental Health
    Care." *Everyday Health*. Everyday
    Health Media, LLC, 29 March 2011. Web. 29 July 2014.

APPENDIX D: A ROUGH GUIDE TO SPECIALISTS

Many of the providers you are likely to encounter are listed in Table 7.

Table 7
Specialists Licensed in the U.S.

Specialist	Typical Problems Treated and Methods Used	Credentials
Agency Affiliated Counselor (AAC)	• Treats mental health issues, addictions • Provides counseling through their employment • Staffs residential programs	• B.A. or B.S. • Must have written supervisory agreement
Certified Advisor (CA)	• As above but less independent • Must have supervisor on site	• Associates Degree • Must have written supervisory agreement
Certified Counselor (CC)	• Treats mental, behavioral, and emotional issues • Treats issues with daily life and making choices • Uses many approaches (see Appendix F)	• B.A. or passage of an exam • Written supervisory agreement required

Specialist	Typical Problems Treated and Methods Used	Credentials
Cognitive Behavior Psychologist	• Treats anxiety, depression, phobias, addictions • Treats mood, psychotic and eating disorders • Assumes problematic behaviors result from maladaptive thinking and beliefs that can be reinterpreted and eliminated with a structured program	• M.S. or Ph.D.
Counselors in Training: Associate Licensed Professional (ALPC), Lic. Associate (LAC), Lic. Associate Mental Health (LACMH), Lic. Associate Professional (LAPC),	• Treats mental, behavioral, emotional issues and disorders • Treats addictions • Treats as licensed professional counselor but with supervision	• M.S. but still in training • Has not yet passed licensure exam • Must have supervisor

Specialist	Typical Problems Treated and Methods Used	Credentials
Limited Licensed Professional (LLPC), Licensed Professional Associate (LPCA), Provisional Professional (PPC)	• Treats mental, behavioral, emotional issues and disorders • Treats addictions • Treats as licensed professional counselor but with supervision	• M.S. but still in training • Has not yet passed licensure exam • Must have supervisor
Developmental Behavioral Pediatrician	• Treats behavioral, regulation and attention disorders • Treats developmental disorders, delays, and disabilities • Can prescribe medication • Treats as pediatrician with additional knowledge of developmental issues	• M.D. with additional training in develop-mental and behavioral pediatrics
Marriage and Family Therapist (MFT)	• Treats relationship and family dynamics, emotional and psychological issues • Use many paradigms, (see Appendix E)	• M.S.

Specialist	Typical Problems Treated and Methods Used	Credentials
Occupational Therapist	• Helps with basic daily life tasks (e.g. tying shoes, dressing) • Helps with motion, strength, nervous system deficits, and coordination	• M.S.
Physical Therapist	• Helps with movement, range of motion, flexibility, balance, posture • Helps with coordination and motor skills	• M.S.
Psychiatrist	• Treats psychiatric, emotional, and developmental disorders • Uses combination of psychotherapy and medication	• M.D. with additional 4-year residency in psychiatry
Psychoanalyst	• Treats emotional, sexual, psychological disorders • Treats issues of character and identity • Treats unconscious thoughts and feelings believed to cause problematic behaviors	• M.S. or Ph.D. or D.O. (Doctor of Osteopathic Medicine)

Specialist	Typical Problems Treated and Methods Used	• Credentials
Speech Pathologist	• Treats language, voice, auditory processing disorders and delays • Treats social and pragmatic language issues	• M.S.

Source: "Licensure Requirements for Professional Counselors." *American Counseling Association: Ethics and Professional Standards.* American Counseling Association, 2010. Web. 20 March 2014.

APPENDIX E: PSYCHOLOGICAL PARADIGMS

Psychology has a number of perspectives, or paradigms, through which problems are viewed. I have attempted to summarize the principal approaches below.

1. Behavioral Psychology (Behaviorism)

This approach grew from work on classical conditioning by the Russian physiologist Ivan Pavlov. Pavlov found that the behavior of dogs could be changed by the introduction of an external stimulus. Influenced by Pavlov, the psychologist John Watson created the behavioral school of psychology with his 1913 lecture and subsequent paper entitled, "Psychology as the Behaviorist Views It." This school remained the primary psychological approach from the early to mid 20th century.

Behavioral Psychology postulates that all human behavior is the result of interactions with the environment. In direct opposition to psychodynamics, there is no consideration of an internal world in behaviorism; all behavior is a response to a stimulus. The work of behavioral psychology is to understand the behaviors that result from a given stimulus, and the stimuli needed to elicit certain behaviors. A subsequent innovation in behaviorism came from B.F. Skinner, who developed the idea of operant conditioning and reinforcement and the school of radical behaviorism. Skinner believed that there is no free will. All behaviors are a result of their own consequences and are either repeated or not, based on the response they get. Operant conditioning using positive reinforcement and punishment is believed to shape behavior

In behaviorism psychology is a science. Stimuli and behavior can be observed and measured. All behavior can be changed with the appropriate conditioning, consisting of positive reinforcement when the desired behavior occurs and negative reinforcement or punishment when it does not. If a behavior is problematic, this approach believes that there is a stimulus that can change it for the better. Once that stimulus is found and introduced, the problematic behavior should be eliminated. This approach has fallen out of favor, but its fundamental tenets are still used today to manage problematic behaviors such as obsessions and compulsions.

2. Biological Psychology (Physiological Psychology, Behavioral Neuroscience, Biopsychology, Psychobiology)

This perspective looks at physical, genetic, and biological origins of human behavior. It seeks to understand how the brain and nervous system influence behaviors and feelings. All behaviors are thought to be the result of biological processes on the level of neurotransmitters and electrochemistry. Biological psychology seeks to answer questions such as which parts of the brain are responsible for which functions. For example, it has been found that two areas of the cerebral cortex affect language. In this approach genetics is considered to be an important factor in behavior. As technology has advanced and brain scans and other diagnostic tools have become available, this perspective has grown in it's understanding of human behavior. Biological psychology continues to be relevant today.

3. Cognitive Psychology

Cognitive psychology replaced behaviorism in what has come to be called the "Cognitive Revolution." It was officially launched as a paradigm by Ulric Neisser in 1967 with a book entitled, "Cognitive Psychology."

This perspective focuses on mental processes such as memory, attention, thinking, perception, language, creativity, and problem solving. It is a scientific approach that believes the key to understanding behaviors and feelings is to understand the flow of information in the human brain. How we store, process, and take in sensory information, regardless of the stimuli, is the basis of all human endeavor in this approach. The function of the human mind is believed to be similar to that of the information processing function of a computer and large computer models have been built to try to understand and mimic brain processes.

Cognitive psychology became dominant in the 1970's. Its scientific methodology continues to struggle with the inherent problems that cognitive processes cannot be measured, are often not observed, and usually occur in extremely short time spans. The advances in this approach have been a result of laboratory experiments and large computer models. Cognitive psychologists today continue to explore brain function, often working with neuroscientists and cognitive scientists.

4. Cross-Cultural Psychology

Cross-cultural psychology aims to study the effects of culture on human psychology. Understanding how different cultural forces influence various behaviors and how the norms of various cultures differ and are similar is the aim of this approach. It is a methodology for studying whether psychological theories hold across cultures. Two distinct cultural groups are studied and compared to determine which psychological theories are universal and why. When cultural groups differ, this approach studies why and how. Cross-cultural psychology is relevant today.

5. Evolutionary Psychology

This perspective looks at which mental processes, traits, and behaviors may have resulted from evolutionary adaptations. For example, evolutionary psychology believes that the language and perception we have today are a result of an evolutionary process. This approach attempts to link psychology to evolution via the idea that various aspects of human functioning exist today because they have given us a reproductive advantage. This perspective is new and still contested.

6. Humanist Psychology (Humanistic Psychology, Humanism)

Humanist psychology became popular in the 1950s as a reaction to the shortcomings of behavioral and psychodynamic psychology. At this time behavioral psychology was seen as too limited by its scientific approach and psychodynamics was felt to focus too strongly on the unconscious, leaving little concern for the conscious mind. Sometimes called the "third force" in psychology, after psychodynamics and behaviorism, this approach brought a new set of values to the understanding of human behavior. Among the important figures in this movement are Carl Rogers, who developed the idea of a client-centered psychology and Abraham Maslow, who created the idea of a hierarchy of needs motivating human behavior.

In humanistic psychology the whole person is considered. Human beings are believed to be intrinsically good and motivated by a drive to achieve their innate potential and creativity and to create meaning and value in their lives. This drive is called self-actualization. Behavior is not predetermined in this approach. Instead human beings are believed to have free will to influence, if not determine, their behaviors. The subjective experience of each individual is considered paramount and psychiatric and social problems are thought to be a result of deviations from the intrinsic drive for self-actualization.

Helping each person to become aware of their unique strengths and goals is the focus of this approach. It is the job of the humanistic psychologist to free any blocks interfering with the drive to self-actualize. This approach is in use today.

7. Psychodynamic Psychology

This perspective grows from Freud's psychoanalytical work in the late 19th century and the subsequent work of Jung, Adler, Klein, and others. In this approach, the interplay of drives and forces, operating mainly in our unconscious, is believed to influence our feelings and behaviors. Memories of early dysfunctional childhood experiences and relationships are thought to reside in our unconscious, creating current day conflicts and problems. The id, the ego, and the superego are all elements of this approach and describe the flow of psychological energy among our unconscious, our conscious, and the external environment. Behavior is thought to be the result of two instinctual drives: one the life and sex drive and the second the death and aggression drive. In this perspective dreams, fantasies, and memories are used to identify early experiences that are believed to have planted the seeds of the conflicts and problems we struggle with today. Once made self-aware through a therapeutic conversation, this approach believes that the patient can then begin to heal.

8. Socio-Cultural Psychology (Cultural Historical Psychology, Activity Theory, Cultural Psychology, Social Development Theory, School of Vygotsky)

Socio-cultural psychology originated with the work of Lev Vygotsky, a contemporary of Freud. His original work was done in the 1920s but due to a ban by Stalin it was not widely read until the 1990s.

In this approach, social and cultural factors are considered important in the development of human behavior and thought. The cultural values, customs, and beliefs taught by adults to children are thought to influence the development of higher brain functioning and to prepare children to join their particular culture as adults. Different cultures are believed to produce psychologically different adults. Social interactions are believed to influence the development of the brain. This perspective has strong implications for education and is considered relevant today.

APPENDIX F: A ROUGH GUIDE TO THERAPIES

The therapies I speak about in this section are psychological, focusing on human thoughts, emotions, behaviors, and the origins of each. Psychological therapies fall roughly into three groupings:

- Behavioral
- Humanistic
- Psychodynamic and Psychoanalytic

Hybrids of these are Integrated Therapy, which brings together theories from a variety of approaches and Eclectic Therapy, in which the therapist draws on whatever therapy is most appropriate to meet a client's needs in the moment. As each of these approaches is significantly different, it is useful to understand what your choices may be.

1. Cognitive Behavioral Therapy (CBT)

This therapy approach views problematic behaviors as originating in erroneous thinking and beliefs. It seeks change by identifying, understanding, and rethinking the dysfunctional behavior and then reinforcing a healthier substitute behavior instead. This therapy assumes that thoughts determine feelings and behavior. If the client's thinking or their relationship to their thinking can be changed, then problematic feelings and behaviors should change as well. Depending on the problem, this therapy may be more cognitive or more behavioral. Depression, for example, would be treated with a more cognitive approach, focusing on identifying and changing distorted thinking. Obsessive-compulsive disorders and phobias would be treated with a more behavioral approach, in which the client is conditioned to replace the problematic obsessive or phobic behavior with a healthier alternative behavior.

2. Dialectical Behavioral Therapy

Dialectical behavioral therapy (DBT) evolved in the 1980s as a modification to cognitive therapy. It is a combination

134

of cognitive behavioral therapy, validation, and mindfulness derived from Buddhist mediation techniques. DBT provides a supportive environment in which clients are made to feel accepted and that their issues and problems make sense and are valid. Emphasis is placed on helping clients understand when their judgments are sound and when they can trust themselves. When change is appropriate, cognitive behavioral techniques are incorporated as well. DBT is practiced with a combination of group and individual therapy sessions. It has been found to help borderline personality disorders, mood disorders, suicidal beliefs, addictions, psychotic disorders, and dysfunctional behaviors. The name dialectical refers to the opposing goals of acceptance and change, which are central to this therapy.

3. Eclectic Therapy

Eclectic Therapy is pragmatic, drawing on techniques from other therapies as needed to address a particular client problem. It does not adhere to any single therapeutic approach and is unique to the individual and their particular problems in that moment. This approach is commonly used today

4. Existential Therapy

Existential therapy is a psychodynamic therapy in which therapists look at human beings as individuals living within the limitations of human existence. It is concerned with the present human condition and seeks to understand the unique experience of "being" for each individual client. The subject of existential therapy is the choices an individual makes when confronted with life's limitations. Each individual is believed to have free will and a responsibility to face his limitations from a physical, psychological, and spiritual perspective. Given the limitations of the human condition, this therapy concludes that life is meaningless. Each client is helped to understand their values and goals. Once made aware of these, the client can hopefully make choices that lead to peace with individual limitations and the inherent meaninglessness of life. In the view of existential therapists, a life well lived is a life of responsibility, awareness and acceptance.

Existential therapy has its origins in the thinking of Soren Kierkegaard and Friedrich Nietzsche in the 19th century. Later Heidegger, Sartre, Camus, and others expanded upon this thinking to include the ideas that man's experience is subjective, there is no universal morality, and individuals need to define their morals and values in this context.

5. Exposure Therapy

Exposure therapy is designed to treat some forms of anxiety. It is a type of behavioral therapy that exposes the client to an ever-increasing intensity of the particular stimuli responsible for their anxiety, while also maintaining a safe environment. For example, clients suffering from a fear of heights might be asked to climb ever-higher stairwells. Over time, the fear response is hopefully broken and the anxiety is eliminated.

6. Expressive Therapies: Art, Music, Dance, Drama, Creative Writing, Poetry, Play, Sandplay, and Imagery

Expressive therapies are an alternative means of therapeutic communication. Each provides a medium in which the therapist works with a client to resolve emotional or other conflicts, such as pain or trauma. Expressive therapies offer advantages over traditional talk therapy for clients who might not otherwise be engaged or able to express themselves well using language. Therapists do not attempt to interpret the therapy sessions but instead encourage self-exploration. Because thoughts and feelings are not exclusively represented in language, expressive therapies are sometimes able to access internal conflicts and issues more easily than talk therapies. Memories in particular are often more easily accessible through expressive therapies.

The multisensory experience of expressive therapy often focuses and energizes clients. Imagination and creativity enter into the therapeutic process and often act to facilitate transformations. Expressive therapies have been shown to have value in early attachment issues, childhood disorders, pain reduction, Alzheimer's disease, other dementias, and autism.

7. Humanistic Therapy

This approach views human behavior as motivated by the drive to achieve one's potential and find meaning in life, which it calls the state of being self-actualized. Individuals are viewed as intrinsically good and having full responsibility for their choices and actions. Humanistic therapy attempts to identify the unique forces acting on a client and the client's unique strengths. It seeks to understand the forces and problems impeding a client's drive to self-actualize. Once understood and resolved, this therapy believes the client can then continue their unique path towards growth and fulfillment unimpeded by problematic thoughts and behaviors.

8. Jungian Psychotherapy (Analytical Psychotherapy)

Jungian therapy is a psychoanalytic therapy that uses the analysis of dreams to understand and integrate the forces of the unconscious mind, the conscious mind, and the ego. This process allows clients to gain insight into emotional problems and to develop coping mechanisms to solve these problems. With this therapy, a higher level of consciousness is believed to be possible. This higher consciousness transforms the psyche to achieve one's maximum potential as a unique individual. The goal of Jungian psychotherapy is to emerge as the true self. Pathology and neuroses, such as addictions or uncontrolled emotional states and behaviors, are seen as valuable in identifying problematic elements of the unconscious and the deeper-seated problems of which we may not be aware. Jungian therapy seeks to put the client in touch with their inner strengths. These strengths are believed to be healing forces that are available to the client in their ultimate quest to realize their potential as human beings. The therapeutic relationship between client and therapist is one of equals, with the therapist guiding the client in a collaborative process that follows the unconscious wherever it may lead them.

9. Psychoanalysis

Psychoanalysis attempts to free problematic emotions and feelings believed to have been formed in early childhood and held in the unconscious. Clients are encouraged to freely associate and speak about dreams and fantasies as a means to bring these repressed emotions and feelings from the unconscious into the conscious mind. The client is helped to gain insight and awareness of these deep-rooted forces, which are thought to drive current day behaviors. Psychoanalysis is an intensive therapy usually requiring four or five sessions per week. It can go on for years.

10. Psychodynamic Therapy

Psychodynamic therapy is a less intense version of psychoanalysis in which the client delves into their unconscious in an attempt to gain self-awareness. While psychoanalysis assumes primal forces such as sex and aggression drive human behavior, psychodynamic therapy assumes that the need for connection and attachment is the primary drive in all of us. An example of a conversation in psychodynamic therapy might be how our relationship with our parents influences the relationships we have today. Psychodynamic therapy can usually be done successfully with one or two weekly sessions.

APPENDIX G: A VERY ROUGH GUIDE TO PSYCHIATRIC MEDICATIONS

Psychiatric or psychotropic medications affect the chemistry of the brain and nervous system to alter feeling, perception, behavior, and thought. These drugs act on chemicals in the brain, typically neurotransmitters or neuroreceptors, to change the electrical signals that pass between brain cells. There is much controversy about the true efficacy of some of these drugs and the extent to which the U.S. pharmaceutical industry influences their use. At a minimum, the psychiatric drugs available to us today are the result of a highly politicized approval process (Mundy).

There are six major classes of psychiatric drugs, each characterized by its effect on the brain. These classes and the primary pediatric conditions for which they are prescribed are:

- <u>Antidepressants</u> – prescribed for major depressive disorder, obsessive compulsive disorder, other anxiety and depression conditions, and involuntary urination.
- <u>Anti-Anxiety Medications (Anxiolytics)</u> – prescribed for various types of anxiety such as obsessive compulsive disorder, phobias and panic.
- <u>Mood Stabilizers (Anti-Manic Agents, Anticonvulsants</u>) – prescribed for disorders of mood, such as mania or depression, that typically occur with bipolar disorder and schizophrenia. (There is some controversy over the effectiveness of mood stabilizer medications for depression.)
- <u>Antipsychotics</u> – prescribed for psychosis, delusions, various types of thought disorders, aggressive and impulsive behavior, and attention disorders.
- <u>Stimulants</u> – prescribed for Attention Deficit Hyperactivity Disorder (ADHD), sleep disorders, and obesity.
- <u>Depressants (Sedatives and Hypnotics)</u> – are prescribed for insomnia, anxiety, sedation, and anesthesia.

The following lists are by no means complete but do provide a context for where commonly prescribed psychiatric medications fall, the potential side effects, and the mechanism through which each class of medication works, to the extent it is known. As medical research and experience with these drugs is always changing, the most effective medications for each condition are constantly changing as well. It is thus essential to double check the latest advice on whatever medication you and your doctor may be considering for your child.

1. Antidepressants

Antidepressant medications affect how we feel, think and behave. They are prescribed to treat depression, anxiety and eating disorders, chronic pain, bipolar disorder, and less often migraines, sleep disorders, attention deficit hyperactivity disorder (ADHD), and addictions.

There is much debate about the efficacy of anti-depressants in the treatment of depression. The medical community seems to agree that for cases of severe depression, antidepressants are helpful. In studies of mild to moderate depression, however, antidepressants often do not show efficacy over placebos (Barbui). If you are considering this type of medication for your child, you should be aware that the FDA has issued its strongest alert for children, adolescents, and young adults on antidepressants. This alert, called a "black-box warning," cautions that there may be an increased risk of suicidal thought and behavior for anyone under age 24 taking antidepressants and advises close monitoring. An important consideration counter to this warning is the disturbing fact that that if untreated, a depressed child, adolescent, or young adult can be at risk for suicide as well.

Antidepressants affect the levels of serotonin, norepinephrine, and dopamine neurotransmitters in the brain. Each class has a slightly different mechanism but all have the net effect of increasing chemical signals in the brain. This increases brain cell communication, which seems to affect depression. Antidepressants are grouped into classes based on the neurotransmitters they affect, and how they affect them. The newer, second generation, classes of antidepressants have fewer

140

side effects and are classified as:

- SSRIs - Selective Serotonin Reuptake Inhibitors
- SNRIs - Serotonin-Norepinephrine Reuptake Inhibitors
- Atypical Antidepressants – newer generation antidepressants that fall outside the SSRI or SNRI classes

Earlier generation classes of antidepressants include:

- Monoamine Oxidase Inhibitors (MAOIs)
- Tricyclics

SSRIs are the first line of treatment for depression, followed by SNRIs and atypicals. Tricyclics have more side effects and are usually prescribed only after the others above have been found ineffective or are not well tolerated. MAOIs typically are the last treatment choice. They have more side effects and react with certain foods, requiring a special diet. For treatment-resistant depression, a combination of an SSRI or SNRI plus an atypical antipsychotic is sometimes prescribed. Commonly prescribed antidepressants by class are listed in Table 8.

Table 8
Commonly Prescribed Antidepressants

Atypical Antidepressants	MAOIs	SNRIs
Avanza	Eldepryl (12+)	Cymbalta
Budeprion	Emsam (12+)	Desfax (18+)
Buproban	Marplan	Effexor
Desyrel	Nardil	Pristiq
Ludiomil (18+)	Parnate	Serzone
Remeron		
Wellbutrin		
Zyban		

Table 8 Commonly Prescribed Antidepressants		
SSRIs	Tricyclics	Others
Brisdelle Celexa Cipralex Cipramil Lexapro (7+)* Lustral Luvox Paxil Pexeva Prozac (8+)* Rexetin Sarafem (8+)* Seroxat Viibryd Zoloft (6+)*	Allegron Amitriptyline Anafranil (10+)* Adapin (12+)* Aventyl Defanyl (18+) Elavil Norpramin Pamelor Pertofrane Prudoxin (12+)* Sinequan (12+)* Surmontil Triptil (12+)* Vivactil (12+)* Zonalon (12+)*	Atypical Antipsychotic Used with an SSRI or SNRI Abilify Risperdal Seroquel Symbyax (10+) Zyprexa Anticonvulsants Klonopin Lamictal * FDA approved for ages noted

Source: Stanford University, "A Guide to Psychiatric
    Medications for Young People." *What Meds.* 2014. Web.
    20 March 2014.

    A number of SSRI and tricyclic antidepressants have
been clinically tested and FDA approved for the treatment of

pediatric depression. All other antidepressants routinely prescribed for children and adolescents, are prescribed based on their efficacy in clinical trials in adults. In 2007, the FDA updated their public alert for antidepressants. The alert now states that for anyone under age 24 antidepressants may cause suicidal thoughts and behavior. This "black box warning" remains in place today. It is based on reviews of clinical trials that found a small increase in suicidal thinking in children and adolescents taking SSRIs for depression. No suicides occurred during the trials and the data in support of this warning is now controversial (Cuffe). As mentioned above, untreated depression can put a child, adolescent, or young adult at risk for suicide as well. The potential side effects of commonly prescribed antidepressants are listed in Table 9.

Table 9
Potential Side Effects of Commonly Prescribed Antidepressants

Atypical Antidepressants	• Agitation, Nervousness • Diarrhea • Dizziness, Lightheadedness • Dry Mouth • Fatigue, Weakness • Headaches • Increased Appetite • Increased Cholesterol and Triglycerides • Increased Heartbeat • Insomnia • Low Blood Pressure • Nausea, Vomiting • Sleepiness • Weight gain

Table 9 Potential Side Effects of Commonly Prescribed Antidepressants	
MAOIs	• Agitation • Anxiety • Change in Mood or Behavior • Constipation, Diarrhea • Drowsiness • Dry Mouth • Fatigue • Headaches • Insomnia • Lightheadedness, Dizziness • Nausea • Weakness • Weight Gain Less Common • Dangerously High Blood Pressure (with certain foods) • Difficulty Urinating • Heart Attacks • Involuntary Muscle Jerks • Liver Inflammation • Low Blood Pressure • Muscle Aches
SNRIs	• Sometimes no side effects • Constipation • Difficulty Urinating • Dizziness • Dry Mouth • Excessive Sweating • Fatigue

Table 9 Potential Side Effects of Commonly Prescribed Antidepressants	
SNRIs (continued)	• Headache • Loss of Appetite • Loss of Sleep • Nausea • Nervousness, Agitation
SSRIs	• Side effects often last only a few weeks • Agitation, Shakiness • Anxiety • Blurred Vision • Constipation or Diarrhea • Dizziness • Drowsiness • Dry Mouth • Feeling or Being Sick • Headaches • Indigestion, Stomach Aches • Loss of Appetite • Sleep Problems • Weight Gain or Loss Less Common • Bruising or Bleeding Easily • Confusion • Hallucinations • Serotonergic Syndrome (panic attacks and nerve cell activity that can be fatal) • Stiffness, Shaking • Suicidal Thinking (danger now contested)

Table 9 Potential Side Effects of Commonly Prescribed Antidepressants	
Tricyclics	• Blurred Vision • Confusion • Constipation • Disorientation • Dizziness • Drowsiness • Dry Mouth • Memory Impairment • Tremors • Urinary Retention • Weight Gain Less Common • Increased Anxiety • Irregular Heart Best
Others	Atypical Antipsychotic + SSRI or SNRI (see Antipsychotics, Table 15 and SSRIs, SNRIs above) Lamictal, (see Mood Stabilizers, Table 13) Klonopin (see Benzodiazepines, Table 11)

Source: "Depression Medications (Antidepressants)." *WebMD*. WebMD, LLC, 2012. Web. 20 March 2014.

2. Anti-Anxiety Medications (Anxiolytics)

Anxiety, or fear, is a response to perceived threat. It is a defensive mechanism that is meant to protect us and enhance survival. When triggered, anxiety causes an increase in arousal, chemical and physiological activity, and a change in behavior. Anxiety disorders result from abnormal regulation in the systems of the brain that control the perception of and defensive response to threat. This results in a distortion of the perceived threat and a disruption in the appropriate level of response.

Anti-anxiety, or anxiety, medications act to reduce the heightened arousal state brought on by anxiety. They depress the central nervous system (CNS), creating a calming, tranquilizing effect that relaxes muscles and decreases restlessness and agitation. The medications commonly prescribed for anxiety fall into four classes plus several others. These classes are:

- Antidepressants
- Benzodiazepines
- Beta-Blockers
- Anticonvulsants (Mood Stabilizers)

Additional medications used to treat anxiety are:

- Agonists
- Antihistamines
- Atypical Antipsychotics
- Buspar
- Nonbenzodiazepine Hypnotics

The mechanisms by which anxiety medications act are not always well understood. Physicians found that antidepressants had an anxiety reducing effect and began prescribing them to treat anxiety. While not yet understanding how antidepressants act to treat anxiety, it is thought that the neurotransmitter serotonin is involved. Benzodiazepines are known to be central nervous system (CNS) depressants. Benzodiazepines increase a neurotransmitter called gamma-aminobutyric acid (GABA), which causes a sedating, sleep inducing, euphoric, and muscle relaxing effect.

Beta-blockers are known to act on beta receptors, which are found in cells in the tissue of the sympathetic nervous system. They block stress hormones such as epinephrine, weakening the stress response and thus reducing anxiety, which is a reaction to perceived stress.

Anticonvulsants, although not yet well understood in this application, are known to decrease excessive neuron activity associated with the fear response in the brain. The antihistamine Hydroxyzine is thought to increase the neurotransmitter GABA, producing a sedating effect, as with the benzodiazepines. Medications commonly prescribed to treat anxiety are listed in Table 10.

Table 10
Commonly Prescribed Anxiety Medications

For Generalized Anxiety Disorder (GAD)		
Antidepressants	Benzodiazepines	Others
Amitril	Ativan (12+)*	Agonists
Adapin (12+)*	Diastat (6 mths)*	Guanfacine
Avanza	Klonopin	Intuniv
Buspar	Librium	Minipress
Catapres	Seroxat	Tenex
Celexa	Valium (6 mths+)*	
Cipralex (12+)*	Valrelease (6 mths+)*	Anticonvulsants
Cipramil	Xanax*	Gabapentin
Cymbalta (7-17)*		Lyrica
Desyrel		Neurontin
Dohme		
Effexor		
Elavil		
Emitrip		
Endep		*FDA approved
Enovil		for ages noted

Table 10 Commonly Prescribed Anxiety Medications		
For Generalized Anxiety Disorder		
Antidepressants (continued)	Benzodiazepines	Others (continued)
Etrafon Kapvay Lexapro (12+)* Levazine Ludiomil Lustral Luvox Lyrica (7-17)* Marplan Nardil Paxil Pexeva Prozac (8+)* Prudoxin (12+)* Remeron Sarafem Seroxat Sharpe Sinequan (12+)* Tofranil Viibryd Zoloft Zonalon (12+)*		Atypical <u>Antipsychotics</u> Mellaril Risperdal Saphris Seroquel Stelazine <u>Beta-Blockers</u> Inderal <u>Others</u> Ambien Buspar <u>Antihistomines</u> Atarax Benadryl Hydroxyzine Vistaril
		*FDA approved for ages noted

Table 10 Commonly Prescribed Anxiety Medications		
For Obsessive Compulsive Disorder (OCD)		
Antidepressants	Benzodiazepines	Others
Anafranil (10+)* Avanza Brisdelle Celexa Cipralex Cipramil Cymbalta Effexor Lexapro Lustral (6+)* Luvox (8+)* Nardil Paxil Pexeva Prozac (7+)* Remeron Sarafem (7+)* Seroxat Tofranil Zoloft (6+)*	Xanax	<u>Agonists</u> Depade <u>Anticonvulsants</u> Topamax Atypical <u>Antipsychotics</u> Risperdal Symbyax (8+) Zyprexa
		*FDA approved for ages noted

Table 10 Commonly Prescribed Anxiety Medications		
For Panic Disorder		
Antidepressants	Benzodiazepines	Others
Adapin	Klonopin	<u>Anticonvulsants</u>
Avanza	Librium	Gabapentin
Aventyl	Xanax	Neurontin
Brisdelle		
Celexa		Atypical
Cipramil		<u>Antipsychotics</u>
Desyrel		Symbyax (10+)
Effexor		
Lustral		
Luvox		
Nardil		
Norpramin		
Pamelor		
Parnate		
Paxil		
Pexeva		
Pristiq		
Prozac		
Prudoxin		
Remeron		
Sarafem		
Seroxat		
Sinequan		
Tofranil		
Zoloft		
Zonalon		

Table 10 Commonly Prescribed Anxiety Medications		
For Phobias		
Antidepressants	Benzodiazepines	Others
Brintellix Celexa Effexor Lexapro Lustral Luvox Nardil Parnate Paxil Pexeva Prozac Seroxat Viibryd Zoloft	Ativan Diastat Klonopin Librium Niravam Valium Xanax	<u>Anticonvulsants</u> Lyrica Neurotin <u>Antihistomines</u> Benadryl Vistaril <u>Beta-Blockers</u> Inderal Innopran Tenormin <u>Other</u> Ambien Buspar

Table 10 Commonly Prescribed Anxiety Medications		
For Post Traumatic Stress Disorder (PTSD)		
Antidepressants	Benzodiazepines	Others
Adapin	Ativan	Agonists
Celexa	Serax	Catapres
Cymbalta	Valium	Guanfacine
Desyrel	Xanax	Minipress
Effexor		Tenex
Lexapro		
Lustral		Anticonvulsants
Luvox		Depakote
Manerix		Depakene
Nardil		Gabitril
Paxil		Lamictal
Pexeva		
Prozac		Antihistamines
Prudoxin		Benadryl
Remeron		Vistaril
Serax		
Seroxat		Antipsychotics
Serzone		Abilify
Sinequan		Invega
Wellbutrin		Risperdal
Zoloft		Seroquel
Zonalon		Symbyax
		Zyprexa
		Beta-Blockers
		Inderal

Table 10 Commonly Prescribed Anxiety Medications		
For Social Anxiety Disorder		
Antidepressants	Benzodiazepines	Others
Effexor Lustral Luvox Manerix Nardil Paxil Pexeva Prozac Seroxat Zoloft	Ativan Klonopin Xanax	Anticonvulsants Gabapentin Neurontin

Source: "Introduction- Common Medications for Anxiety
    Disorders." *anxieties.com*. The Anxiety Disorder
    Treatment Center of Durham and Chapel Hill, NC, n.d.
    Web, 20 March 2012.

As discussed in an earlier section, the FDA issued its strongest warning for antidepressants after clinical trials found a small percentage of children, adolescents, and young adults taking SSRIs had increased thoughts of suicide. This alert still stands, even though no suicides have occurred. Other, less disturbing, side effects of anxiety medications differ by class. Benzodiazepines, also referred to as anti-anxiety medications, commonly cause dizziness and drowsiness and must be prescribed for short-term use only. The long-term use of benzodiazepines can lead to dependence and a withdrawal syndrome when one does stop. Beta-blockers are not advised for children with asthma or diabetes as symptoms of these illnesses could worsen. Buspar has many of the same side effects as benzodiazepines but is usually not addictive. Several generic forms of Buspar were pulled from the U.S. market but this was not due to safety concerns. The possible side effects for commonly prescribed anxiety medications are listed in Table 11.

Table 11
Potential Side Effects of Commonly Prescribed Anxiety Medications

Agonists	(see Sedative-Hypnotics, Table 19)
Anticonvulsants	(see Mood Stabilizers, Table 13)
Antidepressants	(see Antidepressants, Table 9)
Antihistamines	• Blurred Vision • Diarrhea, Constipation • Dizziness • Drowsiness • Dry Eyes, Dry Mouth • Fatigue • Headache • Inability to Empty Bladder • Mental Disturbances (Confusion, Moodiness, Restlessness) • Nausea, Vomiting Less Common • Insomnia • Nightmares • Rapid Heartbeat • Tightness of Chest
Atypical Antipsychotics	(see Antipsychotics, Table 15)

Table 11 Potential Side Effects of Commonly Prescribed Anxiety Medications	
Benzodiazepines	• Confusion • Decreased Coordination • Decreased Respiratory Function (dose related) • Dependence (with long term use) • Drowsiness, Sedation • Impaired Memory • Relaxing of Muscles • Weakness Less Common • Blurred Vision • Change in Appetite • Change in Heart Rate • Depression or Euphoria • Headaches • Lack of Inhibition • Loss of Orientation • Nausea • Nightmares
Beta-Blockers	• Often no side effects Less Common • Constipation or Diarrhea • Dizziness • Fatigue • Headache • Insomnia • Nausea • Shortness of Breadth

Table 11 Potential Side Effects of Commonly Prescribed Anxiety Medications	
Beta Blockers (continued)	Less Common • Upset Stomach
Others **should not be prescribed for children with kidney or liver disease	Ambien (see Sedative-Hypnotics, Table 19) Buspar** • Headaches • Nervousness • Restlessness • Vomiting Buspar - Less Common • Blurred Vision • Cramps • Diarrhea • Dizziness • Insomnia • Lightheadedness • Muscle Pain • Nightmares • Spasms • Strange or Vivid Dreams • Tremors • Weakness

Source: "Benzodiazepines." *Wikipedia.* Wikipedia Foundation, Inc., 28 March 2014. Web. 28 March 2014.; "Beta-Blockers." *Wikipedia.* Wikipedia Foundation, Inc., 25 March 2014. Web. 28 March 2014.; "Buspar." *Wikipedia.* Wikipedia Foundation, Inc., 25 March 2014. Web. 28 March 2014.

3. Mood Stabilizers

Mood stabilizers treat disorders of mood, which are also called affective disorders. Mood disorders in which mood is excessively depressed are called major depressive disorder, clinical depression, or unipolar depression. Alternatively, mood may be excessively euphoric or manic, or it may alternate between depressed and manic, which is called bipolar disorder. At each extreme, mood is disproportionate to the surrounding reality. It is hypothesized that mood disorders may in part be an evolutionary adaption. Depressed or lowered mood may increase coping skills in times of stress. A hyper-vigilant, manic mood may increase focus and concentration in times of threat. The cause of mood disorders is not well understood, although an imbalance in the neurotransmitter levels of serotonin, dopamine, and epinephrine in the brain is thought to be involved.

Medications prescribed to treat mood disorders are called mood stabilizers. These medications attempt to flatten the extremes of mood to a more stable equilibrium state. They fall into four classes:

- Anticonvulsants
- Antidepressants
- Lithium
- Antipsychotics

In addition, the combinations below are sometime used:

- Antidepressant + Lithium or Anticonvulsant
- Antidepressant + Anticonvulsant
- Antidepressant + Antipsychotic (bipolar disorder)
- Antidepressant + Buspar (depressive mood disorders)

How these medications work to stabilize mood is not completely understood. Anticonvulsants were first developed to treat epilepsy but were found to also stabilize mood. The mechanism for this is thought to be an increase in the neurotransmitter GABA, which stabilizes electrical activity in the brain. Excessive electrical activity in the brain has been observed with mood disorders. Atypical antipsychotics and lithium are thought to affect the chemical neurotransmitters serotonin and dopamine in the brain, which affect mood. Antidepressants similarly act by affecting neurotransmitters, as discussed in an earlier section. Commonly prescribed mood stabilizers are listed in Tables 12a and 12b. It is worth noting that the FDA has not yet approved a mood stabilizer for children under age 10.

Table 12a
Mood Stabilizers Commonly Prescribed for Bipolar Disorder

Anticonvulsants	Antidepressants	Others
Atretol	Adapin	Agonists
Carbatrol	Emsam (12-17)	Catapres
Depacon*	Ludiomil	Kapvay
Depakene*	Marplan	Mirapex
Depakote*	Nardil	
Epilim	Prozac	Atypical
Episenta	Prudoxin	Antipsychotics
Epival	Sinequan	Abilify (13-17)**
Epitol	Viibryd	Geodon
Gabitril		Invega
Equetro		Latuda
Lamictal		Risperdal (10+)**
Neurontin		Saphris**
Tegretol		Seroquel (10+)**
Topomax		Sycrest**
Trileptal*		Symbyax
		Zyprexa (13+)**
*must monitor blood levels **FDA approved for ages noted		

Table 12a Mood Stabilizers for Bipolar Disorder		
Antidepressants (continued)	Lithium*	Others (continued)
Wellbutrin Zonalon Zyban	Eskalith** Lithobid**	<u>Benzodiazepines</u> Ativan Klonopin Razepam Restoril Temaz Valium Buspar <u>Sedative-Hypnotics</u> Ambien Lunesta Rozerem Sonata <u>Stimulants</u> Ritalin *must monitor blood levels **FDA approved for ages 3-17

Source: "Mood Stabilizers for Child and Teen Bipolar Disorder." *WebMD*. WebMD, LLC, 10 April 2013. Web. 20 March 2014.

Table 12b
Mood Stabilizers Commonly Prescribed for Major Depressive Disorder (MDD), Persistent Depressive Disorder (Dysthymia), Seasonal Mood Disorders and Other Disorders of Mood

Antidepressants	Atypical Antipsychotics	Others
Adapin*	Abilify*	Anticonvulsants
Allegron	Geodon	Lamictal
Amitril*	Invega	
Amitriptyline*	Risperdal	Others
Avanza	Saphris	Buspar**
Aventyl	Seroquel	Lithium
Budeprion	Zyprexa	
Buproban		Stimulants**
Celexa		Adderall
Cipralex (9+)*		Ritalin
Cipramil		
Cymbalta		
Desfax		
Desyrel		
Dohme*		
Elavil*		
Emitrip*		
Endep*		
Enovil*		
Etrafon*		
Levazine*		
Lexapro (9+)*		
Ludiomil		
Lustral		*FDA approved
Luvox		for ages 12+ or
Nardil		for ages noted
Pamelor		** Prescribed
Parnate		with an
Paxil (adolescents)		antidepressant

Table 12b Mood Stabilizers Commonly Prescribed for MDD, Dysthymia, etc.		
Antidepressants (continued)	Atypical Antipsychotics	Others
Pexeva (adolescents) Pristiq Prozac (8+)* Prudoxin Remeron Sarafem (8+)* Seroxat Serzone Sharpe* Sinequan Viibryd Wellbutrin Zoloft Zonalon Zyban		*FDA approved for ages 12+ or for ages noted

Source: Trevor L. Young, "What exactly is a mood stabilizer?"
Journal of Psychiatry and Neuroscience 29:2 (2004): 87-
88. Print.

The side effects associated with mood stabilizers vary
with the individual medication. The FDA has issued a warning
that anticonvulsants may cause an increased risk of suicidal
thought and behavior. While issuing this warning, the FDA has
not recommended that patients stop using these drugs.
Psychiatrists point out that the risk of suicide from untreated
bipolar disorder is often greater than the noted medication risks.
Lithium, Depakote, and Depakene require frequent blood tests to
monitor for potential thyroid and liver damage. If caught early,

any such damage can easily be reversed by lowering of the dosage. Potential side effects of commonly prescribed mood stabilizers are listed in Table 13.

Table 13
Potential Side Effects of Commonly Prescribed Mood Stabilizers

Anticonvulsants	• Anorexia • Confusion • Dizziness • Drowsiness • Headaches • Nausea • Loss of Appetite • Loss of Coordination • Skin Rashes • Sun Sensitivity • Vomiting Less Common • Bruising or Bleeding • Hair Loss • Potential Liver Damage* • Stomach pains • Suicidal thoughts and behavior • Tremors • Weight Gain
* can be avoided with routine blood tests to monitor liver function	
Antidepressants	(see Antidepressants, Table 9)
Atypical Antipsychotics	(see Antipsychotics, Table 15)
Lithium	• Acne • Hair Loss • Increased Thirst • Increased Urination

Table 13 Potential Side Effects of Commonly Prescribed Mood Stabilizers	
Lithium (continued) *Can be avoided with regular blood tests to monitor liver and thyroid function	• Loss of Coordination • Memory Loss • Nausea • Tremors • Weight gain Less Common • Change in Vision • Drowsiness, Fatigue • Hallucinations • Muscle Weakness • Potential Liver and Thyroid Damage* • Restlessness • Skin rashes • Slurred Speech
Others	Adderall, Ritalin (see Stimulants, Table 17) Catapres, Mirapex (see Agonists, Table 19) Buspar (see Anti-Anxiety Medications, Table 11) Klonopin (see Anti-Anxiety Medications, Table 11)

Table 13 Potential Side Effects of Commonly Prescribed Mood Stabilizers	
Others (continued)	Lithium (see Lithium above) Lamictal (see Anticonvulsants, above)

Source: "Mood Stabilizers for Child and Teen Bipolar
Disorder." *WebMD*. WebMD, LLC, 10 April 2013. Web.
20 March 2013.

<u>4. Antipsychotics (Neuroleptics)</u>

Antipsychotic medications are used across a broad range
of conditions. They treat psychosis, schizophrenia, delusions,
hallucinations, and disordered thinking. They are also prescribed
for symptoms arising from autism, anxiety, depression, and
ADHD. They treat disorders of personality, mood, eating
(anorexia, bulimia), and disruptive behavior. The first generation
"typical" antipsychotics were introduced in the 1950s. More
recently a second generation of "atypical" antipsychotics was
released.

Both generations of antipsychotics work by blocking the
neurotransmitter dopamine. Atypical antipsychotics also block
the neurotransmitter serotonin. The precise mechanism by which
these medications work is not known, but it is known that
dopamine and serotonin affect mood, emotion, sleep, and
regulation. The newer atypical antipsychotics were thought to
have fewer side effects but this is now challenged. Physicians
note that there is little evidence for superior efficacy, or for
fewer side effects with the atypicals (Jauhar). Commonly

prescribed antipsychotics are listed in Table 14.

Table 14
Commonly Prescribed Antipsychotic Medications*

First Generation "Typicals"	Haldol Haldol Decanoate Loxitane Orap (ages 12+) Moban Navane Prolixin Serentil Stelazine Thorazine Trilafon
Second Generation "Atypicals" * Many are FDA approved for adolescent schizophrenia, bipolar disorder, hyperactivity, irritability, and severe behaviors	Abilify Clozaril (16+) Fanapt Geodon Invega Latuda Risperdal Saphris Seroquel Solian Sycrest Symbyax Zyprexa

Source: "Introduction to Mental Health Medications." *NIH* National Institute of Health. Web. 23 March 2014.

The potential side effects of antipsychotics are frightening. These are powerful drugs with potentially life changing and permanent side effects. The decision to use such medications must weigh the benefits carefully against the risks. Certainly these medications are indicated when psychotic or psychotic-like symptoms exist, as ongoing, unmitigated psychosis runs the risk of becoming permanent. Potential side effects of commonly prescribed antipsychotics are listed in Table 15.

Table 15
Potential Side Effects of Commonly Prescribed Antipsychotics

Typical Antipsychotics	Atypical Antipsychotics
• Diabetes • Drowsiness • Flattening of Affect • Involuntary Movements • Loss of Attention • Loss of Ability to Experience Pleasure • Loss of Will • Metabolic Disorders • Passivity • Permanent Movement Disorders (Tardive Dyskinesia) • Restlessness • Rigidity • Tremors • Uncontrollable Muscle Contractions • Weight Gain	• Blurred Vision • Constipation • Cognitive Impairment • Dizziness, Drowsiness • Heart Attacks • Hypotension • Inability to Experience Pleasure • Loss of Affect • Loss of Attention • Loss of Will • Metabolic Disorders • Permanent Movement Disorders (Tardive Dyskinesia) • Rapid Heartbeat • Seizures • Skin Rashes • Sun Sensitivity • Uncontrollable Muscle Contractions • Urine Retention • Weight gain

Table 15 Potential Side Effects of Commonly Prescribed Antipsychotics	
Typical Antipsychotics	Atypical Antipsychotics (continued)
	Additional Side Effects for Clozaril • Heart Attacks • Inflammation of heart muscle • Low white blood cell count • Seizures

Source: "Introduction: Mental Health Medications." *NIH.*
National Institute of Mental Health, n.d. Web. 23 March
2014.

5. Stimulants

Stimulants are used to treat attention disorders (ADHD), impulsivity, hyper-activity, narcolepsy, apathy, lethargic states of being, and executive function issues. These medications increase brain activity by increasing arousal and improving mental and physical function. Stimulants also produce heightened awareness, focus, concentration, alertness, vigilance, wakefulness, and enhanced sensation. They increase endurance and enhance movement. They can induce a euphoric state. Stimulants can also cause insomnia and psychotic symptoms in some cases. They may also increase the risk of obesity.

Simulants increase activation in the frontal lobes of the brain. Many classes of drugs and substances fall under this title, making stimulants difficult to classify. Examples include amphetamines, caffeine, phenethylamines, methylphenidate, and extracts from certain plants. Examples of commonly prescribed stimulants, and non-stimulants prescribed to treat ADHD, are listed in Table 16.

Table 16
Commonly Prescribed Stimulants*

Amphetamines, Dextroamphetamines, Lisdexamfetamine	Adderall Dexedrine Dextrostat Dyanavel Evekeo ProCentra Vyvanse
Methylphenidates, Dexmethylphenidates	Concerta Daytrana Focalin Metadate Methylin QuilliChew Quillivant Ritalin
Non-Stimulants Prescribed to treat ADHD	Agonists Catapres Intuniv Kapvay Tenex Antidepressants Aventyl Effexor Lexapro Nardil Norpramin *Most are FDA approved for pediatric ADHD

Table 16 Commonly Prescribed Stimulants*	
Non-Stimulants Prescribed to treat ADHD	<u>Antidepressants</u> Pamelor Parnate Pertofrane Tofranil Wellbutrin Zoloft <u>Antipsychotics**</u> Abilify Risperdal Seroquel Zyprexa <u>Others</u> Buspar Strattera *Most are FDA approved for pediatric ADHD **Often prescribed with a stimulant

Source: "Stimulant." *Wikipedia*. Wikipedia Foundation, Inc., 24 March 2014. Web. 28 March 2014.

The commonly seen side effects of stimulants are relatively benign. The most serious of these is a suppression of growth, which is uncommon. Children for whom this class of medication is prescribed should have their grow rate monitored. Potential side effects of commonly prescribed stimulants are listed in Table 17. Most result from the increase in arousal state caused by these medications.

Table 17
Potential Side Effects of Commonly Prescribed Stimulants

Physiological Effects	Psychological Effects
• Abdominal Pain	• Agitation
• Chest Pain	• Anxiety
• Decreased Appetite	• Apathy
• Dizziness	• Depression
• Headaches	• Hallucination (at doses above
• Jitteriness	recommended level)
• Liver Damage (Strattera)	• Inattention
• Nausea	• Irritability
• Reduced Growth Rate (rare)	• Manic Symptoms
• Stomach Aches	• Moodiness
• Sleep Disturbances	• Nervousness
• Tics	• Psychosis
• Sudden Repeated Tremors	• Social Withdrawal
• Vomiting	
• Weight Gain	

Source: "Stimulants." *Palo Alto Medical Foundation.* Sutter Health. October 2013. Web. 20 March 2014.

6. Sedative-Hypnotics
Sedative-hypnotics are principally used to treat sleep disorders, reduce anxiety and aggression, as anesthesia, and to treat seizures. It is important to note that the use of sedative-hypnotics in children and adolescents is not well researched and the level of knowledge and confidence in the efficacy, tolerance, dosing,

and safety is minimal.

Sedative-hypnotic medications act to depress central nervous system activity. Sedatives are anxiolytics, producing calm and reducing anxiety. Hypnotics have a stronger effect on the nervous system, producing drowsiness and bringing on and maintaining sleep. The extent to which these medications depress central nervous system activity is directly related to dosage. Increasing the dosage level of a sedative can create hypnotic effects. Increasing the dosage level of a hypnotic creates an anesthesia medication, and if increased further, coma. In many cases, these medications act through the neurotransmitter GABA to inhibit central nervous system activity, which then decreases arousal and excitement.

Sedative- hypnotic medications fall into two main classes:

- Benzodiazepines
- Barbiturates

In addition, the following other classes of medication are prescribed, to act as sedatives:

- Agonists
- Antidepressants
- Antihistamines
- Herbal Supplements (Melatonin)
- Nonbenzodiazepines

Today, with a few exceptions, barbiturates have largely been replaced by benzodiazepines. The barbiturate phenobarbital is still prescribed for anesthesia and as an antiseizure medication in children and adolescents. Methohexital and amobarbital barbiturates are used in diagnostic testing for psychotic and epileptic disorders. Beyond these uses, barbiturates are not considered appropriate for children and adolescents.

While many of the sedative-hypnotic medications have been FDA approved for adults, few have been approved for children. Melatonin, a popular herbal sedative, for example, is not FDA regulated at all. The safety and purity of various formulations of melatonin may vary widely, causing effectiveness and side effects to vary widely as well. The long-term effects of daily use are unknown. Chloral Hydrate, which was at one time popular, has been largely abandoned due to its serious potential side effects such as cardiac disease and renal dysfunction. The agonists Tenex and Catapres are routinely prescribed as sedatives for children, but have not been FDA approved for children, nor do they have clear dosing guidelines. Commonly prescribed sedatives and hypnotics are listed in Table 18.

Table 18
Commonly Prescribed Sedative- Hypnotics

Agonists	Barbiturates	Benzodiazepines
Catapres Intuniv Kapvay Tenex	Dexmedetomidine Etomidate Methohexital Pentobarbital Phenobarbital Propofol	Ativan* Dalmane Diastat Halcion Razepam Restoril Temaz Valium Valrelease Versed Xanax
Antidepressants	Antihistomines	
Adapin Amitril Amitriptyline Avanza Desyrel Dohme	Benadryl* Dramamine Hydroxine Unisom (12+)	* FDA approved for insomnia ages 12+

Table 18 Commonly Prescribed Sedative-Hypnotics		
Antidepressants (continued)	Antihistomines (continued)	Nonbenzodiazepines
Elavil Emitrip Endep Enovil Etrafon Levazine Prudoxin Remeron Sharpe Sinequan SolTab Viibryd Zonalon	Vallergan	Ambien Lunesta Sonata
Herbal Supplements	Others	
Chamomile Kava-Kava Lavender Melatonin Valerian	Chloral Hydrate Iron Supplements Prosom Rozerem**	**new class of hypnotic, FDA approved for adult insomnia

Source: Bantu Chhangani, Donald E. Greydanus, Dilip R. Patel and Cynthia Feucht. "Pharmacology of Sleep Disorders in Children and Adolescents." *Pediatric Clinics of North America* 58:1 (2011): 273-291.

Potential side effects of sedative-hypnotics reflect the effects of a depressed nervous system and are shown in Table 19.

Table 19
Potential Side Effects of Commonly Prescribed Sedative-Hypnotics

Agonists	• Constipation • Dizziness • Drowsiness • Fatigue • Headaches • Lightheadedness • Light Sedation • Weakness
Antidepressants	(see Antidepressants, Table 9)
Antihistomines	(see Anti-Anxiety Medications, Table 11)
Barbiturates	• Coma (in overdose) • Decreased Respiratory Function (dose related) • Dependence • Dizziness • Drowsiness • Seizures • Suppressed REM Sleep

Table 19 Potential Side Effects of Commonly Prescribed Sedative-Hypnotics	
Benzodiazepines	• Addiction • Amnesia • Confusion • Decreased Cardiovascular and/or Respiratory Function (dose related) • Dependence • Drowsiness • Impaired Coordination • Impaired Memory • Loss of Inhibition • Relaxation of Muscles • Sedation • Weakness
Herbal Supplements	• Side effects not well documented
Nonbenzodiazepines	• Amnesia • Depression • Possible Increase in Cancers and/or Tumors • Strange Behaviors
Others	Chloral Hydrate • Arrhythmias • Cardiac Failure • Drug Dependence • Gastrointestinal Problems • Liver Failure

Table 19 Potential Side Effects of Commonly Prescribed Sedative-Hypnotics	
Others (continued)	<u>Chloral Hydrate (continued)</u> • Nausea • Renal Failure • Skin Rashes • Vomiting <u>Prosom</u> • Amnesia, Forgetfulness • Blurred Vision • Depression • Dizziness • Drowsiness • Headache • Loss of Balance or Coordination • Muscle Weakness • Numbness, Tingling, or Burning Feeling in Muscles <u>Rozerem</u> • Depression • Dizziness • Drowsiness • Insomnia • Possible Endocrine System Impact • Unusual Thoughts <u>Somnote</u> • Diarrhea • Dizziness

Table 19 Potential Side Effects of Commonly Prescribed Sedative-Hypnotics	
Others (continued)	Somnote (continued) • Drowsiness • Nausea • Skin Rashes • Stomach Pain • Unsteadiness • Vomiting

Source: Bantu Chhangani, Donald E. Greydanus, Dilip R. Patel and Cynthia Feucht. "Pharmacology of Sleep Disorders in Children and Adolescents." *Pediatric Clinics of North America* 58:1 (2011): 273-291.

7. Medications Prescribed in an Off-Label Use

Off-label use refers to medications approved by the FDA for one condition that have been found to be helpful in treating something else as well. These medications can be prescribed for this second condition, although they are not FDA approved for this use. There are many examples of off-level usage across many conditions and classes of medications. Selected examples are listed below in Table 20.

Table 20
Selected Mediations Prescribed in an Off-Label Usage

Medication	Condition Approved to Treat	Off-Label Uses
Klonopin	• Panic Disorder • Seizures	• Depression • Migraines • Moderate Anxiety

Table 20 Selected Mediations Prescribed in an Off-Label Usage		
Medication	Condition Approved to Treat	Off-Label Uses
Neurontin	• Seizures	• Phobias • Psychotic Ideation • Psychosis • Social Anxiety
Risperdal	• Bipolar Disorder • Irritability • Schizophrenia	• Anxiety • Depression • OCD • Panic • Post Traumatic Stress
Ritalin	• ADHD	• Bipolar Disorder • Depression
Seroquel	• Bipolar Disorder • Schizophrenia	• Anxiety • Depression

Table 20 Selected Mediations Prescribed in an Off-Label Usage		
Medication	Condition Approved to Treat	Off-Label Uses
Symbyax	• Depression	• Anxiety
Topamax	• Migraines • Seizures	• OCD • Panic
Zyprexa	• Bipolar Disorder • Psychotic Conditions • Schizophrenia	• Depression • OCD • Social Anxiety

Source: Kelli Miller. "Off-Label Prescription Drug Use: What You Need to Know." *WebMD*. WebMD, LLC, 2009. Web. 20 March 2014.

A summary of the psychiatric medications described in these appendices, by type, is shown below in 21.

Table 21
Summary of Commonly Prescribed Psychiatric Medications

1=Anxiety Medication 2=Antidepressant 3=Antipsychotic 4=Mood Stabilizer 5=Stimulant (ADHD) 6=Sedative-Hypnotic	1	2	3	4	5	6
Abilify		✓	✓	✓		
Adapin	✓	✓		✓		✓
Adderall					✓	
Allegron		✓				
Alprazolam	✓					
Ambien	✓					✓
Amitril		✓		✓		✓
Amitriptyline		✓		✓		✓
Amobarbital						✓
Anafranil	✓	✓				
Atarex	✓					
Ativan	✓					✓
Avanza	✓	✓		✓		✓

1=Anxiety Medication 2=Antidepressant 3=Antipsychotic 4=Mood Stabilizer 5=Stimulant (ADHD) 6=Sedative-Hypnotic	1	2	3	4	5	6
Aventyl	✓	✓		✓		
Benadryl	✓					✓
Benzedrine					✓	
Brisdelle	✓	✓				
Budeprion		✓		✓		
Buproban		✓		✓		
Buspar	✓			✓		
Catapres	✓			✓		✓
Celexa	✓	✓		✓		
Chamomile						✓
Chloral Hydrate						✓
Cipralex		✓				
Cipramil	✓	✓		✓		
Clozaril			✓	✓		
Concerta					✓	
Cymbalta	✓	✓		✓		

1=Anxiety Medication 2=Antidepressant 3=Antipsychotic 4=Mood Stabilizer 5=Stimulant (ADHD) 6=Sedative-Hypnotic	1	2	3	4	5	6
Dalmane						✓
Daytrana					✓	
Depacon				✓		
Depade	✓					
Depakene	✓			✓		
Depakote	✓			✓		
Desfax		✓				
Desoxyn					✓	
Desyrel	✓			✓		✓
Dexedrine					✓	
Dextrostat					✓	
Diastat	✓					✓
Diazepam	✓					
Dohme	✓	✓		✓		✓
Dramamine						✓
Dyanavel					✓	

1=Anxiety Medication 2=Antidepressant 3=Antipsychotic 4=Mood Stabilizer 5=Stimulant (ADHD) 6=Sedative-Hypnotic	1	2	3	4	5	6
Edronax				✓		
Effexor	✓	✓		✓		
Elavil	✓	✓		✓		✓
Eldepryl		✓				
Elvanse					✓	
Emitrip	✓	✓		✓		✓
Emsam		✓		✓		
Endep	✓	✓		✓		✓
Enovil	✓	✓		✓		✓
Epilim				✓		
Episenta				✓		
Epival				✓		
Equetro				✓		
Eskalith				✓		
Etrafon	✓	✓		✓		✓
Evekeo					✓	

1=Anxiety Medication 2=Antidepressant 3=Antipsychotic 4=Mood Stabilizer 5=Stimulant (ADHD) 6=Sedative-Hypnotic	1	2	3	4	5	6
Fanapt			✓			
Focalin					✓	
Gamanil		✓				
Geodon			✓	✓		
Halcion						✓
Haldol			✓			
Haldol Decanoate			✓	✓		
Hydroxyzine	✓					✓
Inderal	✓					
Innopran	✓					
Intuniv	✓					✓
Invega			✓	✓		
Kapvay	✓				✓	
Kava-Kava						✓

1=Anxiety Medication 2=Antidepressant 3=Antipsychotic 4=Mood Stabilizer 5=Stimulant (ADHD) 6=Sedative-Hypnotic	1	2	3	4	5	6
Klonopin	✓	✓		✓		
Lamictal	✓	✓		✓		
Latuda			✓	✓		
Lavender						✓
Levazine	✓	✓		✓		✓
Lexapro	✓	✓		✓		
Librium	✓			✓		
Lithium				✓		
Lithobid				✓		
Loxitane			✓			
Ludiomil	✓	✓		✓		
Lunesta						✓
Lustral	✓	✓		✓		
Luvox	✓	✓		✓		

1=Anxiety Medication 2=Antidepressant 3=Antipsychotic 4=Mood Stabilizer 5=Stimulant (ADHD) 6=Sedative-Hypnotic	1	2	3	4	5	6
Lyrica	✓					
Manerix	✓					
Marplan	✓	✓		✓		✓
Melatonin						✓
Metadate					✓	
Methohexital						✓
Methylin					✓	
Minipress	✓					
Mirapex				✓		
Moban			✓			
Nardil	✓	✓		✓		
Navane			✓			
Neurontin	✓			✓		
Niravam	✓					
Norpramin	✓	✓		✓		

1=Anxiety Medication 2=Antidepressant 3=Antipsychotic 4=Mood Stabilizer 5=Stimulant (ADHD) 6=Sedative-Hypnotic	1	2	3	4	5	6
Orap			✓			
Pamelor	✓	✓		✓		
Parnate	✓	✓		✓		
Paxil	✓	✓		✓		
Pertofrane	✓	✓				
Pexeva	✓	✓		✓		
Phenobarbital						✓
Pristiq	✓	✓		✓		
ProCentra					✓	
Prolixin			✓			
Prosom						✓
Prozac	✓	✓		✓		
Prudoxin	✓	✓		✓		✓
QuilliChew					✓	

1=Anxiety Medication 2=Antidepressant 3=Antipsychotic 4=Mood Stabilizer 5=Stimulant (ADHD) 6=Sedative-Hypnotic	1	2	3	4	5	6
Quillivant					✓	
Razepam						✓
Remeron	✓	✓		✓		✓
Restoril						✓
Rexetin		✓				
Risperdal	✓	✓	✓	✓		
Ritalin				✓	✓	
Rozerem						✓
Saphris	✓		✓	✓		
Sarafem	✓	✓		✓		
Serax	✓					
Serentil			✓			
Seroquel	✓	✓	✓	✓		
Seroxat	✓	✓		✓		
Serzine	✓					
Serzone	✓	✓		✓		

1=Anxiety Medication 2=Antidepressant 3=Antipsychotic 4=Mood Stabilizer 5=Stimulant (ADHD) 6=Sedative-Hypnotic	1	2	3	4	5	6
Sharpe	✓	✓		✓		✓
Sinequan		✓		✓		✓
Solian			✓			
SolTab	✓					✓
Somnote						✓
Sonata						✓
Stelazine	✓		✓			
Strattera					✓	
Surmontil		✓				
Sycrest			✓	✓		
Symbyax	✓	✓	✓			
Tegretol				✓		
Temaz						✓
Tenex	✓					✓
Thorazine			✓			
Tofranil	✓	✓				

1=Anxiety Medication 2=Antidepressant 3=Antipsychotic 4=Mood Stabilizer 5=Stimulant (ADHD) 6=Sedative-Hypnotic	1	2	3	4	5	6
Topamax	✓			✓		
Trilafon			✓			
Trileptal				✓		
Triptil		✓				
Tyvense				✓		
Unisom						✓
Valium	✓					✓
Valrelease	✓					✓
Venvanse				✓		
Versed						✓
Viibryd	✓	✓		✓		✓
Vistaril	✓					
Vivactil		✓		✓		
Vyvanse					✓	
Wellbutrin		✓		✓		
Xanax	✓					

1=Anxiety Medication 2=Antidepressant 3=Antipsychotic 4=Mood Stabilizer 5=Stimulant (ADHD) 6=Sedative-Hypnotic	1	2	3	4	5	6
Zeldox				✓		
Zipwell				✓		
Zoloft	✓	✓		✓		
Zonalon	✓	✓		✓		✓
Zyban		✓		✓		
Zyprexa	✓	✓	✓	✓		

Source: Stanford University. "A Guide to Psychiatric Medications for Young People." *What Meds*. 2014. Web. 20 March 2014.; "Introduction- Common Medications for Anxiety Disorders." *anxieties.com*. The Anxiety Disorder Treatment Center of Durham and Chapel Hill, NC, n.d. Web, 20 March 2012.; "Mood Stabilizers for Child and Teen Bipolar Disorder." *WebMD*. WebMD, LLC, 10 April 2013. Web. 20 March 2014. "Introduction to Mental Health Medications." *NIH*. National Institute of Health. Web. 23 March 2014.; "Stimulant." *Wikipedia*. Wikipedia Foundation, Inc., 24 March 2014. Web. 28 March 2014.; Bantu Chhangani, Donald E. Greydanus, Dilip R. Patel and Cynthia Feucht. "Pharmacology of Sleep Disorders in Children and Adolescents." *Pediatric Clinics of North America* 58:1 (2011): 273-291.

APPENDIX H: DELAYS AND DISORDERS

I have always wondered how these two conditions differ, so am including an explanation here. A delay means that a child's development is normal but slower then the norm for age. For example, a child who is late to speak might have a speech delay. The child's speech will come eventually but is not following the developmental milestones for age at this point in time. Sometimes therapy is recommended, but delays often can self-correct over time without therapy or intervention.

A disorder is more serious. A disorder means a child's development is abnormal relative to the norm for age. For example, autism is a disorder. A child with autism may never reach many of the developmental milestones, even with extensive therapy and intervention. Whatever it is that is disordered may or may not improve. Therapy is almost always recommended and often medication is as well.

WORKS CITED

"Abilify is the first antipsychotic approved for major depressive disorder." *Pharmacist's Letter*. Therapeutic Research Center, 2014. Web. 7 April 2014.

Aboraya, Ahmed, Eric Rankin, John Collin et al. "The Reliability of Psychiatric Diagnosis Revisited: A Clinicians Guide to Improving the Reliability of Psychiatric Diagnosis." *Psychiatry (Egmont)* 3:1 (2006): 41-50. Print.

"About Therapy." *Network Therapy.com*. Substance Abuse and Mental Health Services Administration (SAMHSA), 2014. Web. 19 March 2014.

Adams, Michal Vannoy. "What is Jungian Analysis? "C.G. *Jung and Jungian Analysis: Archetypes, Dreams, Myths, Imagination*. Michael Vannoy Adams, n.d. Web. 23 March 2014.

"Administrative Law- Food and Drug Law- Eastern District of New York Rejects FDA Limitations on Plan B Emergency Contraception as Arbitrary and Capricious." *Harvard Law Review* 127:4 (2014): n. pg. Print.

"Antidepressant Use in Children, Adolescents and Adults." U.S. Department of Health & Human Services. Web. 23 December 2014.

"Anxiety Disorders." *NIH.* National Institute of Mental Health, n.d. Web. 23 March 2014.

"Anxiolytic." *Wikipedia*. Wikipedia Foundation, Inc., 19 March 2014. Web. 2 April 2014.

"Appropriate Use of Psychotropic Drugs in Children and Adolescents." *magellanhealth.com*. Magellan Health Services, n.d. Web. 7 April 2014.

WORKS CITED

Baldessarini, Ross, Gianni Faedda et al. "Switching of Mood from Depression to Mania with Antidepressants." *Psychiatric Times*. UMB Medeca Network, 8 November 2013. Web. 7 April 2014.

Balt, Steve. "I'm Not That Sure That Psychiatric Medications Work." *KevinMD*. Medpage Today, 25 January 2013. Web. 10 March 2014.

Barbui, Corrado, Andrea Cipriani, Jose Ayuso-Mateos and Mark van Ommeren. "Efficacy of antidepressants and Benzodiazepines in minor depressions: systematic review and meta-analysis." *The British Journal of Psychiatry* 198 (2011): 11-16. Print.

Barnett, W.S. Carolan, J.H. Squires and Clarke K. Brown. "The State of Preschool 2015." *State Preschool Yearbook*. National Institute for Early Education, 2015. Web. 21 July 2014.

"Behavioral Health Treatment Services Locator." SAMHSA. Substance Abuse and Mental Health Services Administration. Web. 30 July 2014.

"Benzodiazepines." *Wikipedia*. Wikipedia Foundation, Inc., 28 March 2014. Web. 28 March 2014.

"Beta-Blockers." *Wikipedia*. Wikipedia Foundation, Inc., 25 March 2014. Web. 28 March 2014.

Bishop, S.J. "Neurocognitive mechanisms of anxiety: an integrative account," Trends in Cognitive Science (2007), doi: 10.1016/j.tics. 2007.05.008.

Boeree, C. George. "Individual, Existential and Humanistic Psychology." *General Psychology*. C. George Boeree, 2003. Web. 22 March 2014.

WORKS CITED

"Buspar." *Wikipedia.* Wikipedia Foundation, Inc., 25 March 2014. Web. 28 March 2014.

Cherney, Kristeen. "Depression Medication List." *Healthline.* Healthline Media. Web. 3 November 2014.

Cherry, Kendea. "Perspectives in Modern Psychology." *about.com Psychology.* About.com, n.d. Web. 18 March 2014.

Chhangani, Bantu, Donald E. Greydanus, Dilip R. Patel and Cynthia Feucht. "Pharmacology of Sleep Disorders in Children and Adolescents." *Pediatric Clinics of North America* 58:1 (2011): 273-291. Print.

Clay, Rebecca A. "A renaissance for humanistic psychology." *Monitor on Psychology* 33:8 (2002): 42. Print.

"Cognitive and Behavioral Therapies." *Counseling Directory.* Site by Memiah Limited, 2014. Web. 19 March 2014.

"Cognitive Psychology: History." *mechanism.ucsd.edu.* International Encyclopedia of the Social and Behavioral Sciences, 2001. Web. 20 March 2014.

"Cognitive-behavioral therapy for obsessive-compulsive disorder." *Advances in Psychiatric Treatment* 13 (2007): 438-446. Print.

"Commonly Prescribed Psychotropic Medications." *NAMI.* National Alliance on Mental Illness, n.d. Web 2 April 2014.

Coupey, Susan M. "Barbituates." *PediatricsinReview.* American Academy of Pediatrics, 1997. Web. 5 April 2014.

WORKS CITED

Cowen, P. J. "Pharmacology for Anxiety Disorders: Drugs Available." *Advances in Psychiatric Treatment* 3 (1997): 66-71. Print.

"Cross-cultural psychology." *Wikipedia.* Wikipedia Foundation, Inc., 22 December 2013. Web. 17 March 2014.

Cuffe, Stephen P. "Suicide and SSRI Medications in Children and Adolescents: An Update." *DevelopMentor.* American Academy of Child & Adolescent Psychiatry, Summer 2007. Web. 9 May 2014.

"Delay and Disorder." *Afasic.org.uk.* Afasic, n.d. Web. 24 March 2014.

"Depression (major depressive disorder)." *Mayo Clinic.* Mayo Foundation for Medical Education and Research, 21 Feb 2014. Web. 21 March 2014.

"Depression Medications (Antidepressants)." *WebMD.* WebMD, LLC, 2012. Web. 20 March 2014.

"Developmental Milestones." *CDC 24/7: Saving Lives, Protecting People.* Center for Disease Control and Prevention, 27 March 2014. Web. 7 July 2014.

"Developmental Screening/Coding Fact Sheet for Primary Care Pediatricians." *aapediatric coding newsletter.* American Academy of Pediatrics, 2014. Web. 7 July 2014.

"Drug Record Anticonvulsant Drugs." *LiverTox.* U.S. National Library of Medicine, 3 April 2014. Web. 10 April 2014.

Dulcan, Mina K. *Dulcan's Textbook of Child and Adolescent Psychiatry.* Arlington: American Psychiatric Publishing, 2009. Print.

WORKS CITED

Ellis, Mary Ellen and George Krucik. "Affective Disorders (Mood Disorders)." *Healthline.* Healthline Networks Inc., 30 May 2013. Web. 7 April 2014.

"Evolutionary Psychology." *Wikipedia.* Wikipedia Foundation, Inc., 26 March 2014. Web. 17 March 2014.

Frese, Federick J. III, Edward Knight and Elyn Saks. "Recovery from Schizophrenia: With Views of Psychiatrists, Psychologists, and Others Diagnosed with this Disorder." *Schizophrenia Bulletin.* Oxford University Press, 2009. Web. 10 March 2014.

Freudenrich, Craig. "How Antidepressants Work." *howstuffworks.* HowStuffWorks, Inc., 2014. Web. 7 April 2014.

Gallin, Stacy. "Psychiatry in Crisis: Humanism vs. Scientific Progress." *huminizingmedicine.org.* The Arnold P. Gold Foundation, 20 September 2013. Web. 24 April 2014.

Gerard, Nathan M. "A diagnosis of conflict: theoretical barriers to integration in mental health services & their philosophical undercurrents." *Philosophy, Ethics and Humanities in Medicine: PEHM* 5:4 (2010): n. pag. Print.

Goldberg, Joseph. Rev. of. "Anxiety & Panic Disorders Health Center." *WebMD.* WebMD LLC, 29 March 2013. Web. 20 March 2014.

Grof, Stanislav. *Beyond the Brain: Birth, Death and Transcendence in Psychotherapy.* Albany: State University of New York Press, 1985. Print.

Grohol, John M. "How Do You Cure Mental Illness?" *PsychCentral.* Psych Central, 26 May 2009. Web. 19 March 2014.

WORKS CITED

---. "What is Exposure Therapy?" *PsychCentral.* Psych Central, 30 Jan 2013. Web. 19 March 2014.

---. "Types of Therapies: Theoretical Orientations and Practices of Therapists." *PsychCentral.* Psych Central, 9 Oct 2013. Web. 18 March 2014.

"A Guide to Disability Rights Laws." *ada.gov.* U.S. Department of Justice, Civil Rights Division, July 2009. Web. 8 May 2014.

Haggerty, Jim. "Antidepressants for Bipolar Disorder." *PsychCentral.* Psych Central, 7 April 2014. Web. 7 April 2014.

Harrison, G. "New or old antidepressants? New is better." *BMJ: British Medical Journal* 309 (1994): 1280-1281. Print.

Higgins, Edmund S and Mark Stork George. *Neuroscience of Clinical Psychiatry: The Pathophysiology of Behavior and Mental Illness.* Philadelphia: Lippincott Williams & Wilkins, 2013. Print.

"Highlights of Changes from DSM-IV-TR to DSM-5." *American Psychiatric Publishing.* American Psychiatric Association, n.d. Web. 10 March 2014.

"Historical Paradigms for Treatment of Serious Mental Illness." *SMI Research Group.* University of Nebraska-Lincoln, n.d. Web. 15 March 2014.

Hill, Tim. "Moods Versus Emotions." *Tim's Blog.* Melbourne Psychology, 4 August 2012. Web. 5 March 2014.

Hirsch, Glenn S. "Guide to Psychiatric Medications for Children and Adolescents." *The Child Study Center.* NYU. Lagone Medical Center, n.d. Web. 10 April 2014.

WORKS CITED

Holy Bible: King James Version. New York: American Bible Society, 1999. Print.

"How Different Antidepressants Work." *WebMD*. WebMD, LLC, n.d. Web. 2 April 2014.

"How much talk therapy do psychiatrists do nowadays!?" *sdn*. The Student Doctor Network, 2013. Web. 8 March 2014.

"Humanistic Therapies*." Counseling Directory*. Site by Memiah Limited, 2014. Web. 20 March 2014.

"Humanistic View & Methods." *ahpweb.org*. The Association for Humanistic Psychology, 2013. Web. 20 March 2014.

"Identifying Infants and Young Children with Developmental Disorders in the Medical Home: An Algorithm for Developmental Surveillance and Screening." *Pediatrics* 118:1 (2006): 405-420. Print.

"Insider's Guide: How to Pay for a Therapeutic Wilderness Program." *Fonthillcounseling.com*. Fonthill Counseling, 2014. Web 30 July 2014.

"Introduction- Common Medications for Anxiety Disorders." *anxieties.com*. The Anxieties Disorders Treatment Center of Durham and Chapel Hill, North Carolina, n.d. Web. 20 March 2014.

"Introduction: Mental Health Medications." *NIH*. National Institute of Mental Health, n.d. Web. 23 March 2014.

WORKS CITED

James, Richard and Burl El Gilliland. "Jungian Therapy." *Companion website material for Theories and Strategies in Counseling and Psychotherapy (Fifth Edition)*. Allyn and Bacon, n.d. Web. 18 March 2014.

Jauhar, Sameer. "Are new drugs for schizophrenia better than old ones?" *The Lancet* 37: 9671 (2009): 1249. Print.

Johnson, Suzanne Bennett. "Medicine's paradigm shift: An opportunity for psychology." *Monitor on Psychology* 43:8 (2012): 5. Print.

Karanges, Emily and Ian S. McGregor. "Antidepressants and Adolescent Brain Development." *Future Neurology* 6:6 (2011): 783-808. Print.

Karceski, Steven. "Exploring the Connection Between Mood Disorders and Epilepsy." *Practical Neurology* (2005): 25. Print.

Kerns, Katie. "6 Cheap Ways to Get Mental Health Care." *Everyday Health*. Everyday Health Media, LLC, 29 March 2011. Web. 29 July 2014.

King, Bryan H. "Psychotropic Medication in Persons with Developmental Disabilities." *lanterman.org.* Frank D. Lanterman Regional Center, n.d. Web. 22 March 2014.

Lane, Richard D. "Is it possible to bridge the Biopsychosocial and Biomedical Models?" *Biopsychosocial Medicine* 8:3 (2014): n.pg. Web. 18 March 2014.

"Laws that Govern Special Education." *Partners for Student Success*. Special School District of St. Louis County, 2008. Web. 9 May 2014.

WORKS CITED

Levin, Aaron. "New Evidence Said to Challenge Psychiatry's

Basic Paradigm." *Psychiatric News*. The American Psychiatric Association, 13 June 2013. Web. 10 March 2014.

"Licensure Requirements for Professional Counselors." *American Counseling Association: Ethics and Professional Standards.* American Counseling Association, 2010. Web. 20 March 2014.

Lieberman, Joseph A. III. "Metabolic Changes Associated with Antipsychotic Use." *Journal of Clinical Psychiatry* 6: supplement 2 (2004): 8-13. Print.

Lopez, Courtney. "Perspectives on Psychology." *Sciences 360*. R.R. Donnelley, 20014. Web. 21 March 2014.

Lorberg, Boris, Judith Owens, Malak Rafia et al. "Sleep Disorder Agents." *Table: FDA Approval Status and Research Evidence Quality - Psychotropic Medications in Children.* American Academy of Child and Adolescent Psychiatry, n.d. Web. 7 April 2014.

Lyon, G. Reid. "Reading Disabilities: Why Do Some Children Have Difficulty Learning to Read? What Can Be Done About It?" *The International Dyslexia Association, Perspectives* 29:2 (2003): 1-4. Print.

Maglione M. et al. "Off-Label Use of Atypical Antipsychotics: An Update." *Comparative Effectiveness Review* 43 (2011): n. pag. Print.

Malchiodi, Cathy A. *Expressive Therapies*. New York: Guilford Press, 2005. Print.

WORKS CITED

Matta, Christy. "Dialectical Behavioral Therapy Understood." *PsychCentral.* Psych Central, 2014. Web.

18 March 2014.

McLeiod, Saul. "Biological Psychology." *SimplyPychology.* SimplyPsychology, 2007. Web. 20 March 2014.

---. "The Medical Model." *SimplyPsychology.* Simply Psychology, 2008. Web. 7 March 2014.

---. "Psychology Perspectives." *SimplyPsychology.* SimplyPsychology, 2007. Web. 20 March 2014.

Miller, Kelli. "Off-Label Prescription Drug Use: What You Need to Know." *WebMD.* WebMD, LLC, 2009. Web. 20 March 2014.

"Models of Mental Health: A Critique and Prospectus." *Serendip.* Howard Hughes Medical Institute, the Whitehall Foundation and the Byryn Mawr Tidepool Project, 2006. Web. 5 March 2014

"Monoamine oxidase inhibitors (MAOIs)." *Mayo Clinic.* Mayo Foundation for Medical Education and Research, 21 June 2013. Web. 23 March 2014.

"Mood Disorders." *healthgrades.* Health Grades, Inc., 7 August 2013. Web. 7 April 2014.

"Mood Stabilizers for Child and Teen Bipolar Disorder." *WebMD.* WebMD, LLC, 10 April 2013. Web. 20 March 2014.

WORKS CITED

"Mood Stabilizers: Side Effects." *Camh Knowledge Exchange*. Center for Addition and Mental Health, 2009 Web. 23 March 2014.

Moreland, C. Scott and Liza Bonin. "Patient Information: Depression treatment options for children and Adolescents." *UpToDate Marketing Professional.* Wolters Kluwer. Print. 13 October 2015.

Mundy, Alicia. "Political Lobbying Drove FDA Process." *WSJ In-Depth*. The Wall Street Journal, 6 March 2009. Web. 14 April 2014.

Muench, John and Ann M. Hamer. "Adverse Effects of Antipsychotic Medications." *American Family Physician* 81:5 (2010): 617-622. Print.

Murphy, Doninic. "Philosophy of Psychiatry." *Stanford Encyclopedia of Philosophy*. Metaphysics Research Lab, Center for Study of Language and Information, Stanford University, 28 July 2010. Web. 10 March 2014.

Murray, Robin and Peter, eds. *The Essentials of Postgraduate Psychiatry*. Cambridge: The Press Syndicate of the University of Cambridge, Third Edition. Print.

"NAMI Mission and Identity Statement." *nami.org*. National Alliance for the Mentally Ill. Web. 2 August 2014.

Neisser, Ulric. *Cognitive Psychology.* New York: Meredith Publishing Company, 1967. Print.

WORKS CITED

New Jersey State Bar Association "The Right to Special Education in New Jersey. " *Education Law Center*, 2008.Web. 15 April 2014.

Nordal, Katherine C. "Where has all the psychotherapy gone?" *Monitor on Psychology* 41:10 (2010): 17. Print.

"On the Medicalization of Our Culture." *Harvard Magazine* 4:23 (2009): n.pag. Web. 10 March 2014.

Owens, Judith A., Carol L. Rosen and Jodi A. Mindell. "Medication Use in the Treatment of Pediatric Insomnia: Results of a Survey of Community-Based Pediatricians." *Pediatrics* 111:5 (2003): e628-e635. Print.

"Pharmacology of Sleep Disorders in Children and Adolescents." *Pediatric Clinics of North America* 58:1 (2011): 273-291.

Pies, Ronald. "Should Psychiatrists Use Atypical Antipsychotics to Treat Nonpsychotic Anxiety?" *Psychiatry (Edgmont)* 6:6 (2009): 29-37. Print.

Pilgrim, David. "The Failure of Diagnostic Psychiatry and Some Prospects of Scientific Progress Offered by Critical Realism." *DxSummit.org.* The Global Summit on Diagnostic Alternatives, 2013. Web. 10 March 2014.

Pn, Shabeel. "Sedative-Hypnotic Drugs." *Slideshare.net.* Slideshare, 7 April 2010. Web. 5 April 2014.

Pilgrim, David. "The Failure of Diagnostic Psychiatry and Some Prospects of Scientific Progress Offered by Critical Realism." *DxSummit.org.* The Global Summit on Diagnostic Alternatives, 2013. Web. 10 March 2014.

WORKS CITED

Pn, Shabeel. "Sedative-Hypnotic Drugs." *Slideshare.net* Slideshare, 7 April 2010. Web. 5 April 2014.

"Preventive Services Covered Under the Affordable Care Act." *HHS.gov/HealthCare*. U.S. Department of Health and Human Services, 27 September 2012. Web. 9 July 2014.

"Psychiatric Diagnosis: Thesis, antithesis, synthesis."

The Economist. The Economist Newspaper Limited, 14 October 2010. Web. 10 March 2014.

"Psychiatric Medication." *Wikipedia*. Wikipedia Foundation, Inc., 26 March 2014. Web. 2 April 2014.

"Psychiatric Medication for Children and Adolescents: Part II – Types of Medications." *Facts for Families*. American Academy of Child & Adolescent Psychiatry, May 2012. Web. 10 April 2014.

"Psychiatrist." *Wikipedia*. Wikipedia Foundation, Inc., 14 January 2014. Web. 15 March 2014.

"Psychoanalytic and psychodynamic therapies." *Counseling Directory*. Site by Memiah Limited, 2014. Web. 5 March 2014.

"Psychoanalytic Therapy." *APSA*. American Psychoanalytic Association, 2014. Web. 5 March 2014.

"Psychodynamic Therapy vs Psychoanalysis." *Living Well, Feeling Good*. Brent Henrikson Blog, 4 January 2012. Web. 21 March 2014.

WORKS CITED

Purse, Marc. "FDA Orders "Suicidal Ideation" Warning on Many Mood Stabilizers." *about.com*. About.com, 12 April 2009. Web. 2 May 2014.

Ramsden, Pamilla. "Defining Abnormal Behavior." *Understanding Abnormal Psychology* Sage Publications, Ltd., 2013. Web. 30 July 2014.

Rise, Caroline. "America's Use of Psychotropic Medications." *Medscape Multispecialty*. Medscape Medical News, 17 Nov 2011. Web. 21 March 2014.

Romito, Kathleen and Lisa S. Weinstock. revs. of "Tricyclic and Tetracyclic Antidepressants for Depression." *WebMD*. WebMD, LLC. 11 January 2013. Web. 2 April 2014.

Ryan, Neal, Vinod Bhatara and James M. Perel. "Mood Stabilizers in Children and Adolescents." *Journal of the American Academy of Child and Adolescent Psychiatry* 38:5 (1999): 529-536. Print.

Saavedra, Christian R., Saavedra L. Gaynes et al. "Appendix A Tables of FDA Approved Indications for First-and-Second Generation Antipsychotics." *Future Research Needs for First-and-Second Generation Antipsychotics for Children and Young Adults*. Rockville: Agency for Healthcare Research and Quality, 2012. Print.

Sammon, Aldan. "The biological approach: the basics." *Psychlotron.org.uk*. Approaches to Psychology: Biopsychology, n.d. Web. 20 March 2014.

WORKS CITED

Schneeweiss, S, A.R. Patrick, D.H. Solomon et al. "Comparative safety of antidepressant agents for children and adolescents regarding suicidal acts." *Pediatrics* 125:5 (2010): 876 - 888. Print.

Schwartz, Alan. "The Selling of Attention Deficit Disorder." *The New York Times* 14 December 2013: n.pag. Web. 5 March 2014.

Scott, Sarah and Annemarie Palincsar. "Sociocultural

Theory." *education.com.* Education. Com, 2014. Web. 17 March 2014.

"Services in Schools for Children with Special Needs: What Parents Need to Know." www.aacap.org. American Academy of Child and Adolescent Psychiatry 83: (2014). Web. 13 July 2014.

Shatkin, Jess P." The Diagnosis & Treatment of Pediatric Depression." New York University School of Medicine.

Singh A.R. and S.A. Singh. "Biological Psychiatry, Research and Industry." *Mana Sana Monographs* Jan-Dec. (2007): n.pg. Web. 19 March 2014.

Smith, Dena T. "The Diminished Resistance to Medicalization in Psychiatry: Psychoanalysis Meets the Medical Model of Mental Illness." *Sage Journals, Society and Mental Health.* American Sociological Association, 10 January 2014. Web. 9 March 2014.

"SSRIs (selective serotonin reuptake inhibitors) - Side Effects." *NHS Choices.* National Health Service, 24, April 2010. Web. 24 March 2014.

WORKS CITED

Stanford University School of Medicine. "Categories of Psychiatric Medications." *What Meds*. 2014 Web 23 March 2014.

---. "A Guide to Psychiatric Medications for Young People. " *What Meds*. 2014. Web. 20 March 2014.

---. "A Guide to Psychiatric Medications for Young People. " *What Meds*. 2014. Web. 20 March 2014

Stanford School of Medicine. "A Guide to Psychiatric Medications for Young People. " *What Meds*. 2014. Web.

20 March 2014.

Steinman, Ira. *Treating the Untreatable*. London: Karnac Books Ltd, 2009. Print.

"Stimulant." *Wikipedia*. Wikipedia Foundation, Inc., 24 March 2014. Web 28 March 2014.

"Stimulants." *Palo Alto Medical Foundation*. Sutter Health, October 2013. Web. 20 March 2014.

Taylor, David H. Personal Interview. April 2013.

"Tricyclic and Tetracyclic Antidepressants for Depression." *WebMD*. WebMD, LLC, 11 January 2013. Web. 2 April 2014.

"Type of Antidepressant Doesn't Affect Teens' Risk from Suicide, Study Finds." *Psychiatric News Alert*. American Psychiatric Association, 21 January 2014. Web. 2 April 2014.

Warner, James. "Clinicians' guide to evaluating diagnostic and screening tests in psychiatry." *Advances in Psychiatric Treatment* 10 (2004): 446-454. Print.

WORKS CITED

Watson, John. "Psychology as the Behaviorist Views It." Columbia University. New York, NY. 24 February 1913. Lecture.

"What is Attention Deficit-Hyperactivity Disorder (ADHD, ADD)?" *NIH*. National Institute of Mental Health, n.d. Web 10 April 2014.

"What is Cross Cultural Psychology?" *about.com*. About.com Psychology, n.d. Web. 17 March 2014.

"What is Eclectic Therapy?" *CRC Health Group*. CRC Health Group, Inc., 2011. Web. 19 March 2014.

Yates, William R. and David Bienenfeld. "Anxiety Disorders." Medscape. *WebMD LLC*. 2014. Web. 13 July 2014.

Young, L. Trevor. "What exactly is a mood stabilizer?" *Journal of Psychiatry and NeuroScience* 29:2 (2004): 87-88. Print.

Zarate, C.A, J.L Payne, J. Sing et al. "Pramipexole for Bipolar II depression in a placebo controlled proof of concept study." Biological Psychiatry 56:1 (2004): 54-60. Print.

ABOUT THE AUTHOR

Susan Hendrie-Marais holds master's degrees in mechanical engineering and business, from Stanford University and the University of Chicago respectively. She also holds a bachelor's degree in physics from Smith College. She has been a member of the scientific staff at the Charles Stark Draper Laboratory and the MIT Lincoln Laboratory. She has worked as a strategic consultant with Le Montecatini Edison S.p.A and as a management consultant with Bain & Company and McKinsey & Company. More recently she was one of a small group of founders of The Oak Hill School, a school for special needs children in Marin County. Susan lives in Mill Valley, California and is the mother of a 23-year old son.

INDEX